Aspects *of* Georgetown

My heartfelt gratitude to Ruth Saxe, deus ex machina extraordinaire, for her helpfulness, kindness and patience in shaping this book. To Maxwell MacKenzie and Marianne Michalakis I owe an equal debt of gratitude for their forbearance, cheerful professionalism and good will. This enterprise would not have happened without all of them; I am indeed fortunate.

ISBN 0-9761220-0-6
Flaneur Press
1530 30th Street N.W., Washington, D.C. 20007

These essays first appeared in slightly modified form in the newsletter of
the Citizens Association of Georgetown,

Cover photographs © Maxwell MacKenzie

Ruth MacKenzie Saxe, Editor
Marianne Michalakis, Production & Design

Printed in the United States of America

Contents

Aspects *of* Georgetown

Reflections on what has been called
"the most civilized neighborhood in the world."

By Edith Schafer

Flaneur Press

Ways of Seeing
"The Most Civilized Neighborhood"

THE great Yale architectural historian Vincent Scully said "Put the right words together with the visual facts so that all of a sudden sparks fly and a new skill is born — the ability to see."

"Why," a visitor asked in amazement, "does that house down the street have all those turrets and towers? It looks like it belongs somewhere else." Why indeed. What is it doing here? After all, we live in this darling little stage-set Federal village, don't we? Everyone is in knee breeches and bonnets, aren't they? Children rolling hoops, stately brick houses with fanlights above the front doors, gas lights, a few chickens in the streets...

So, what are all those turrets and towers doing on so many houses? Maidens in pointy hats and wimples should be yearning out of them toward troubadours, toward green and gold unicorns in flowery meads. These Italianate turrets do not make us think of doughty turn-of-the-nineteenth-century Federal ladies in black bombazine. What is going on here?

"*Know thyself*" it says above the entrance to the Delphic Oracle, so the better to do this we consulted a resident oracle, and here's what Georgetown's world-renowned architect Hugh Newell Jacobsen had to say: "The turrets are Richardson Romanesque, very popular in 1885. Richardson was the architect for the John Hay and Henry Adams Houses on Lafayette Square, now torn down. There are only some 25 buildings in Georgetown that are Federal, and maybe three or four that are Colonial. Everything else is pretty much early Eisenhower or late Truman. Coca-Cola Colonial. Our little village is on a domestic scale, and what makes it work is the transfer of lines from one building to another, horizontal lines; follow the heavy lines and you'll see it. It's just houses, little teeny houses and great big houses sitting right next to each other, broken up every once in a while, as they should be, with a monumental building like the post office."

Some other Jacobsen observations:

The Federal Period was roughly 1810 to 1840, but it was a style that hung on. There is no indigenous architecture in America; it all started out with pattern books imported from abroad. The only indigenous architecture in America is the tepee. We are always looking for an American style.

Historic districts want only the status quo. Architects don't believe in the status quo.

The former Bliss house (after they moved out of Dumbarton Oaks) on the corner of 28th and Q still has its old original roof under the new roof. The Blisses were superstitious and believed that if you tore down a house and built a new one on the site, it would be haunted, so they kept the old roof — thus symbolically keeping the old house.

From Q Street down to the river, 28th Street was known as Herring Hill. Everybody sold seafood. The yards are full of oyster shells to this day. Oyster shells and blue and white china.

Architecture is memorable only when it is irrational and expresses the human condition. Beauty is irrational.

Georgetown is a hands-on, tactile place. (Look at the doorknobs.) It is the most civilized neighborhood in the world. You can walk everywhere. It's only seven miles away from the airport. Those foolish enough to move away always move back.

So take that, doubters and skeptics.

– *May 1996*

Life Under the Canopy
Linden, Ginkgo, Maple, Elm

CONSIDER for a moment if you will our beautiful trees. The lovely old elms on Q Street make it a leafy tunnel of green in summer. The elm is perhaps the quintessential American tree. But no, maybe the maple is. What else smolders and glows red-orange against the autumn sky like a sugar maple? The little leaf linden sports enchanting and delicate green heart-shaped leaves. And then there is the noble ginkgo, a true fossil tree, merely 150 million years old. It lets go its intense yellow leaves all at once, usually in early November, leaving us to shuffle through streets of golden fan-shaped confetti like guests at some cosmic wedding.

Is spring coming? Look at the buds on the lindens. They are ready and waiting. Soon the ground will be carpeted with samaras, the winged fruit of the elms and maples.

But enough rhapsodizing, back to business. Here in Georgetown we have our causes and our enthusiasms, and we care, a lot of us care. Beyond that, some of us stand up and are counted. We do something. Do you know about Trees for Georgetown? It's time for everyone to know about it.

When it became apparent that the District government was no longer able to support its once outstanding tree program, Georgetown residents formed a volunteer committee, Trees for Georgetown. Its purpose is to plant and maintain the trees lining our residential streets. Since its inception in 1989, Trees for Georgetown has raised, from among us, tens of thousands of dollars. This money has gone to plant and prune street trees and to remove old tree stumps — and to do this much more economically than could individual homeowners.

First a survey of the 2600 residential tree boxes was undertaken by a licensed arborist. He identified each tree, noted its size and condition, then suggested priorities for maintenance, providing cost estimates.

Then new trees were planted, stumps and dead trees were removed, and a major pruning effort was undertaken to improve the appearance and condition of mature trees.

The District designates which species of tree can be planted on each block, thus assuring through the years a visually pleasing and consistent streetscape. Trees for Georgetown follows the District's master plan, using slightly larger trees than it specifies. Each new tree is 12 to 14 feet tall and has a trunk diameter of two to three inches. Half the soil in the tree box must be changed. A time-release fertilizer capsule is planted with each new tree. Trees are staked, guaranteed for a year and watered their first summer by the nursery contractor. After that we need to water them ourselves in dry summers and mulch them to conserve moisture.

Street trees are under considerably more stress than woodland trees, and their life span is shorter, usually less than 20 years. Each year 30 to 40 of our street trees will die. So every spring now, Trees for Georgetown undertakes a new fundraising effort and, as its coffers refill, begins another round of tree planting.

"Money," said Emerson, "which represents the prose of life, and which is hardly spoken of in parlors without an apology, is, in its effects and laws, as beautiful as roses." Or trees.

– February 1997

Portal, Fanlight, Lintel, Sill

SUNLIGHT slanting through the tall windows where Jefferson dined, where Lafayette danced. Places, our places. George Washington, dining at the Forrest Marbury House at 3550 M Street. That was on the 29th of March 1791. Uriah Forrest had invited President Washington, landowners and the District Commissioners for a discussion of the future Federal city. The Marbury name is associated with a later owner involved in a complicated lawsuit, Marbury v Madison (1803), in which it was ultimately decided that the Supreme Court could declare laws passed by the Congress unconstitutional.

We live in a historic district. Much remains, but much has been taken. The Corcoran Mansion and the Union Tavern, which had played significant roles in our early history, were demolished. The Francis Scott Key House by Key Bridge was torn down. And in the early 20th century, fine old buildings in the commercial area were "modernized," razed or allowed to deteriorate.

For a long time, we took our history for granted. Then, as time and lack of vigilance continued to threaten our treasures — indeed threaten the character of our neighborhood — those residents who were paying attention came to feel that the time had come to talk about preservation.

Charleston, Alexandria and New Orleans all had historic districts protected by law. Why shouldn't Georgetown? Why not indeed? Discussions led to the formation of a committee by the Progressive Citizens Association of Georgetown. Tentative wording of a bill to be introduced into Congress was formulated. The strong endorsement of both citizens' associations in Georgetown was persuasive. An impressive list of witnesses testified in favor of the bill. There was practically no opposition, although some of the longtime black families in Georgetown wondered if this was part of an effort to remove them. They were assured it was not the intent of the bill. Rather, the creation of a Georgetown Historic District was necessary to save some of the fine old architecture in an area that was laid out in 1751.

Essentially, the bill required that all permit requests for construction, alteration or demolition in the historic district be reviewed by the Fine Arts Commission for recommendations as to "the architectural features, height, appearance, color and texture of the materials of exterior construction which is subject to public view from a public highway."

The Old Georgetown Act was enacted on September 22, 1950. It continues to protect us, but vigilance, unfortunately, is still necessary. A unique house on O Street was demolished not long ago, in spite of the strong protests of many. Constant incursions by workers without permits have to be fought off. "It takes a lot of citizen action to make sure people don't get away with things," said J. Carter Brown, Chairman of the Fine Arts Commission, last year at a Citizens Association meeting.

As we mark the fiftieth anniversary of the Old Georgetown Act, how can we be anything but grateful for what we have: our most agreeable mix of grand and small houses, the stylish details of our facades, and our magnificent streetscape of which we are, and should be, justly proud.

– September 2000

Remembering Black Georgetown

THE silent shuttered past, the past of myth and memory. There is a fascination with things that were and will not come again. The air is full of voices and birds, light and shadow.

It is old here, not old like Europe, but old like America, which is getting to be old enough. Waves of generations. Sometimes we think our time is the only real time, but it isn't, it isn't. Think of what has taken place here. Lafayette on horseback fording Rock Creek where the P Street bridge is now. Louisa May Alcott tending the wounded at the Union Hotel Hospital at 30th and M Streets after the terrible carnage at Fredricksburg. A slave auction house at the corner of O and Wisconsin.

A shudder runs through us. The history of black Georgetown is as moving as it gets.

Our little community was a thriving colonial port in the middle of the 18th century. Slaves were imported to handle the region's extensive tobacco crop, and even then the colonists could hardly keep up with the European demand for it. Soon Georgetown acquired a reputation for its slave trade. While the harsher aspects of slavery tended to be muted in the border states, testimony to broken families and ruined lives can be found in the parish registers here.

"Sold off" or "Taken away" can be found next to the names of parishioners of the Mount Zion United Methodist Church at 27th and P Streets. A vault in the Old Methodist Burying Ground (now Mount Zion Cemetery) at 27th and Q overlooking Rock Creek is said to have been a stop on the underground railroad carrying slaves north to Canada.

By the end of the 18th century, Georgetown consisted of about 7,360 souls, of which 2,400 were Negroes; the ratio of slaves to freedmen being about two to one. The times were prosperous, a prosperity which did not really filter down to the black population. Even the worship of God was impeded by separate entrances and seating areas — usually in the balcony — and the refusal of white ministers to baptize black infants. This led to mass baptisms in Rock Creek — a practice which continued into the 20th century — and the founding of the black churches, major presences in the life of African Americans.

These churches still exist: First Baptist, Mount Zion United Methodist, Jerusalem Baptist, Alexander Memorial Baptist, Epiphany Catholic. They were the core and integument of family life. But where are the parishioners that used to live here? Not here anymore. Now these are commuter churches.

In the 1860's Georgetown had a vibrant, stable and self-sustaining black community. In the area east of Wisconsin Avenue known as Herring Hill, historical records give us this glimpse of the life:

"Wisps of smoke from little cookfires in narrow backyards, pigpens, cowsheds, small two-story frame dwellings, barking dogs in the yard. . . paths leading along a dirt road up to old Mt. Zion Church and beyond to the Methodist Cemetery. . . all combined to endow this compact region of fifteen blocks with the air of a close village community."

The years after the Civil War saw the rise of new leadership in the black community. Alfred Pope became a local real estate magnate. He participated in the political life of the community, representing Georgetown before Congress in the matter of merging with Washington. His house at 2900 P Street still stands. In 1873, the Reverend Patrick J. Healy, S. J. became the President of Georgetown University, the first black president of a predominately white university.

Employment opportunities were declining. Nevertheless, in addition to skilled laborers and domestics, there were three prominent doctors, two pharmacists, a respected mortician and many black owners of small businesses. As for the makeup of the community, some wealthy white families had moved into Georgetown, and some, such as the Peters of Tudor Place, had always been here. Georgetown living was a mix of races and classes. Segregated, but it worked.

More later about this significant aspect of our Georgetown history.

8

The Church of Two Worlds

THERE is a large and somewhat mysterious gray brick building on Q Street just east of 31st. It has asymmetrical towers, ebullient little Gothic spires and an air of solidity. It's a church — The Church of Two Worlds. Just what does that mean? What goes on there?

The literature there informs us that Spiritualism is a belief system, not a religion, that "Spiritualism is the Science, Philosophy and Religion of continuous life, based upon the demonstrated fact of communication — by means of mediumship — with those who live in the spirit world." Spiritualists believe that there is no death (except of the body) and that there are no dead.

Entering the church in the early evening of a winter's night, you will find it quiet and empty. On second glance, you'll see a light coming from a half-open door to the right of the lectern, and there in a back room, are maybe ten people sitting around a table. They are immediately pleasant and friendly to a newcomer. A training session for psychics is about to begin.

The leader explains that everyone has psychic ability but that in some people it needs to be encouraged and brought along, allowed to ripen. Psychic ability enables a person to receive and transmit messages. As there is no death, the body is simply left behind, and the spirit goes to another place. It is possible to talk to those who have undergone the change called death, and messages can be received from them. This is reassuring, one of the purposes of mediumship — a medium being one whose organism is sensitive to vibrations from the spirit world and is able to convey messages.

The session begins. We are told to sit comfortably with our legs uncrossed and our feet flat on the floor and to breathe deeply. Three minutes of silence go by. Now we are ready to call upon our guardian angel or spirit guide. We focus on ourselves and ask for enlightenment — for emotional and spiritual growth, to be a finer human being. We surround ourselves with white light. Now we may ask questions of someone in this world, or the other world, preferably questions that do not require a yes or no answer. Some of the participants share their experiences.

We are seeking to achieve clairvoyance, heightened sensitivity, being attuned to the vibration of things, seeing with the mind's eye. Spiritualists believe (don't we all?) that we use just a fraction of what our minds are capable of and that people create veils that prevent them from seeing clearly. Spiritualists try to go beyond the veil to the extraordinary.

Once a month, instead of psychic training, their time together is devoted to the transmission of messages — through psychics or mediums — from those who are no longer in this world, One component of spiritualism is the work of spiritual healing. This is done primarily by the laying on of hands, but healing of the absent works, too, even if the individual doesn't know that healing thoughts are being sent.

"We're glad you are here," a pleasant young man said. "We want people to know that we are not crazy." They are definitely not crazy, just willing to push the edges of the envelope further than most of us.

Spiritualists seem to be skilled in dealing with the challenge of death, common to us all, and from which there are no exceptions.

So the noncommittal gray brick building on Q Street in Georgetown, The Church of Two Worlds, no longer seems so mysterious. But of course, the mystery remains. Let's be perfectly clear, the Mystery remains.

– January 2001

10

What is past, and passing and to come

TIME, the ever-rolling stream, is about to bear venerable St. John's Church on O Street into its third century. The bicentennial celebration that will take place in 1996 and the plans for renovation of this neighborhood treasure serve to stir up the past and remind us again how much history lies about us in Georgetown. Go down underneath the calm and handsome nave and there, clearly visible now, are the stone foundations. The original beams rest right on the hard clay soil. One could be in the Catacombs or underneath Chartres — there is the same sense of those who have gone before, and a sensation of something like awe. There were people who built this and cared about it a long time ago, and now we take up their work. The past with its messages and promises seeps up.

Georgetown, having been chartered in 1751, was already a mercantile community of long standing when work on St. John's began in 1796. William Thornton designed a Federal-style, almost square, church with a tower in front. In 1797, two walls had been built when an economic slump, caused by over-speculation in land took place, and construction stopped.

George Washington died in 1799. In 1800, the Capital in its tangible form, was put on barges in Philadelphia and moved to Washington. Of course, the city of Washington didn't really exist yet, consisting as it did of unfinished buildings draped in scaffolding, muddy unpaved roads and fetid malarial swamps.

In 1801, Jefferson became President. Money was again raised for St. John's, and by 1803 the church had four walls and was closed in. By 1806, it was finished. A rector was hired, the Reverend

John Johnson Sayres, Jr. He and Thornton would walk from Georgetown to Washington to examine the progress of another of Thornton's projects, the Capitol. One can see them in the mind's eye in their period dress, walking the raw, empty thoroughfares of the yet-to-be-built town.

Founders and benefactors who helped build St. John's included the Reverend Walter Dulany Addison, Thomas Hyde, Thomas Corcoran, Benjamin Stoddert and Francis Scott Key, who was a lay reader. Jefferson was purported to have given $50 to St. John's as he did to several other local churches in accordance with his belief that churches were essential to the fabric of the new country.

In 1803, Jefferson effected the Louisiana Purchase (financed by Barings Bank, of recent memory), and in that same period, Lewis and Clark were poking around out West. It was a time of expansion, mirrored by what was going on at St. John's. In 1853, a belfry was added to the tower; in 1864, the parish hall was built; and in 1870, the exterior appearance of the church was changed from Georgian to Victorian. Later, in order to waterproof it, the building was stuccoed and restored to a modified Georgian style. That's where it is today.

All of this, as they say, is history. Now ambitious plans are underway for a much-needed modernization — structural, mechanical and electrical work, handicapped access, elevators, offices and a multipurpose choir room. A handsome three-story atrium will connect the church and the parish hall. The Chapel of the Carpenter will be relocated, as will the Columbarium.

It is an exciting time and an exciting project. Those long ago founders would approve. So will those who will plan the tricentennial a hundred years from now. For we, too, are waist deep in time's ever-rolling stream, in the words of the great hymn, and history itself is both very long and as short as the watch that ends the night.

– March 1995

Written in the Bright Book of Life

"HISTORY," said James Joyce's Stephen Daedalus, "is the nightmare from which I am trying to awake." He was talking, of course, about poor tormented Ireland with its doomed romantic heroes and unspeakable tragedies. For us, living here at the upper end of navigation on the Potomac River, history seems rather more friendly. We, too, have had our heroes and lovers, our eccentrics, patriots and lost causes, and we still have our beautiful houses. They are part of the furniture here.

Enjoy our past. When the world wearies, and perspective on it is needed, proceed to the Peabody Room at the Georgetown Library and throw yourself into history. Your guide there will be Bob Lyle, who knows *everything*. Like the griots of Africa who retain in memory the whole history of their tribe from its earliest origins, Bob Lyle is a walking, talking repository of our past. If he doesn't have every bit of information in his head, he has books and maps and yellowing incunabula that will reveal the histories of our houses and illuminate the passage of the years.

Our houses are storied. Baron de Bodisco, who was Envoy Extraordinaire and Minister Plenipotentiary of the Emperor of all Russia, lived at 3322 O Street in the 1840's. He fell in love with and married a 16-year old local schoolgirl, much to the dismay of her parents. "Beauty and the beast," they cried. One pictures him in thigh-high boots and fur hat, cutting a Muscovite swath in Martin Van Buren's Washington. He and his young wife were happy on O Street. But after he died in 1854, the Bodisco House was divided into 11 apartments and became a slum. It's a slum no more.

13

Samuel Davidson built big, beautiful Evermay, according to the plaque there, between 1792 and 1794. (Plaques are often inaccurate, says Bob Lyle; it was probably a little later.) To keep malefactors away, Davidson put a sign on Evermay which read: "Take care, enter not here, for punishment is ever near." This was an early version of today's security system.

Halcyon House, 3400 Prospect Street, was built by Benjamin Stoddert, first Secretary of the Navy. Around 1900, an eccentric, Albert Adsit Clemons, bought the property and started adding on. Clemons thought that if he kept on building he would never die. He died anyway.

There is a plaque on the "Yellow Tavern" at 1524 33rd Street informing us that Jefferson met with notables there and Lafayette dined on reed birds. One likes to think about the great Frenchman enjoying his sauvignon blanc and the small succulent birds. It's not entirely his fault reed birds these days are in short supply.

The land confiscated to create Georgetown in 1751 was taken largely from two owners, George Beall and George Gordon. There were Indians here at the time, but they didn't look on land as something one owned. Thus was Georgetown coopered together and came into existence as a port. But this was something of a scam because, for complex reasons, it didn't actually go to the river.

If you want to know more about this, or anything else about our village — or if you just want to have your life enriched — go to the Peabody Room at the Georgetown Library. There, history lives.

— November 1995

Provenance and the Life of Things

IN the movie *Out of Africa* when Meryl Streep (Isak Dinesen) arrived in Nairobi with trunks and bales and boxes full of her household effects, we see her at the railroad station, fussing over the fate of her beloved "things." Robert Redford (Denys Finch-Hatton) whom she sees there for the first time, is much amused. Amused, we are given to understand, that she cared so much for her possessions. We are not particularly amused; we understand completely.

Things seem to matter somehow. Do we not see ourselves in heaven, clutching our favorite dinner plates? (Can't bear to part with them.) What about those charming French candlesticks, a bright little kilim, an old silver picture frame, *objets*, all our glorious *tchotchkes*, the props and accoutrements that create the stage set for our interesting lives?

But let's cut to the chase. We have, in Georgetown, two major sources for "things." They aren't specifically antique shops, although we have a lot of those, too. At the Thrift Shop (on P Street near 27th, across from the Seven-Eleven) and the Christ Child Opportunity Shop (on Wisconsin Avenue, just below P), we can indulge our fantasies and do good at the same time. There are so many reasonably-priced treasures in these shops the mind fairly reels. And like all good antiques, these things have provenance, a history.

The Thrift Shop is the more diverse and eclectic. It carries more clothes — some dashing high class stuff that fairly walks out of there — and is full of people. rather like the neighborhood bar in TV's "Cheers," according to a staffer. One Saturday they had to change the window display three times as the merchandise was sold out of it. Upstairs are the consignment items where the choicest goodies are: a big, handsome reproduction serving spoon ($10), a double chafing dish good as new, some stylish small silver candlesticks. On the light side, there are pith helmets and furs — the kind with faces that used to chase each other around ladies' shoulders — perfect for the dress-up box.

The Christ Child Opportunity Shop, too, is always full of people and benefits from its prize location on Wisconsin just below P Street. Repeat customers from all over the country and abroad have discovered it, and rightly so. Upstairs are mouthwatering life enhancers: serving dishes with covers, etched wine glasses, rainbow-hued vases with the light coming through them, wooden kitchen tubs from France, great quilts and irresistible estate jewelry. And armor, yes armor, conquistador style. You, too, can look like Cortez.

Both of these shops take items either as straight donations or on consignment. All profits from donations as well as a percentage from consignment transactions go to support local hospitals and charities, most of which aid sick children. Both shops are staffed by volunteers who give their time gladly to these wonderful enterprises.

This is truly a win-win situation. Once you stop by, you will think, "I must come back again next week. Hmm, wonder what I missed last week?" Visit!

– January 1996

Thank You, Miss Loulie!
Montrose Park, Then and Now

ON February 2, 1936, the *Washington Star* reported that Montrose Park "now faces severe development into an athletic play center or rehabilitation into a nature sanctuary. Residents are confronted with two somewhat divergent, possibly antagonistic, lines of development of the area: one purely recreational, the other playground-athletic. The two can exist side by side, but there is danger of each encroaching upon the other."

The article went on, "The Georgetown Citizens Association vigorously opposed the abolition of the playground, and a compromise was reached." No doubt a compromise will be reached in the present brouhaha, too, even though feeling ran high at the recent meeting. As citizens we are certainly not spineless, supine or shy. This time around, the impetus for a new playground came from a citizens group, the Friends of Montrose Park. The National Park Service liked their proposal and held a meeting to discuss it with the community. Although the new plan is posted at the park, some residents complained that not enough publicity or notice had been given.

The proposed kidney-shaped play area to the right of the big oak tree elicited a strong negative response from the tree and green space lovers, and there were quite a few. The site was regarded as interfering with the grassy sweep of that part of the park, which is clearly visible from R Street. Opponents were quick to point out that the sun would be relentless there in the summer, and therefore the kids wouldn't use it anyway. Some objected to the fencing, some to the proposed rubber-like surface that would be put down inside the fence, some to lack of respect for the grand old tree.

The pro-playground faction cited the outdated equipment, concerns about lead paint, the unsanitary sandbox, the need for a fenced area to contain small children and deter running dogs. They want the play area out where it can be seen, not tucked away behind hedges. (The good news is that there are many more children in Georgetown then there were a few years ago.)

A little history lends perspective to the present *contretemps*. We are fortunate indeed to have Montrose Park, and we almost didn't. From 1837 until 1904, the land was owned by the Boyce family. There was a big house on R Street and various outbuildings scattered about the property. The ropewalk, which predates the Boyces, ran along the side of the house and extended 900 feet back to the gardener's cottage. It's still there. Mrs. Boyce's rose garden was famous and always open to the public. There was a tennis court, a croquet lawn and the boxwood maze and pergola, all still there.

By the turn of the century, the property had fallen into sad disrepair and was slated for development. Enter Sarah Louisa Rittenhouse (Miss Loulie), a woman of vision and determination, who wanted a park for Georgetown. She galvanized women, some 500 of them, to petition Congress and then lobby fiercely to create a park. In 1906, Congress obliged.

So we are lucky to have Montrose to fight over. A wit has defined this present difficulty as a struggle over the rights of trophy kids vs. the rights of treehuggers. They didn't talk that way in 1936, but the issues haven't changed much. Karen Leder of the Friends of Montrose Park says, "We are looking for common ground, which includes preserving vistas, insuring we have a safe playground, meeting the needs of the community."

Georgetowners, despite a tendency toward combativeness, generally work things out.

– October 1996

18

The Brickyard Hill House of Peter Square

IT seems strange to us to put an incinerator into a residential district, even in 1932. But then, what kind of a residential district was Georgetown then? Its Federal past was a distant memory of faded grandeur, its lively New Deal renaissance not yet stirring. From that shabby down-at-the-heels mix of small sleepy businesses, struggling government workers' apartments, converted slave houses, poor crowded alleys and a rendering plant, no one would have thought to cry "NIMBY!"

Even so, the builders were determined to build a handsome upscale incinerator, one to make the neighborhood proud. Reflecting a modern approach to the architecture of public works, they used patterned brickwork, geometric limestone panels and tall industrial steel windows. Good materials were used throughout. It was a handsome Art Deco incinerator.

In recent decades, no longer in use, it had become an embarrassing eyesore with broken windows and barbed wire, a home for the derelict. And right here on the river in the heart of Georgetown! We anguished over it. Ideas for new uses came and went, but no action. Finally an ambitious development began to take place at what we have now learned to call "the incinerator site" — the block bounded by 31st, K and Wisconsin — to include a "multiplex" theater, condominiums and a ritzy hotel. Then a problem of historical preservation intervened.

Nearby, at the top of the site on South Street, stood a very small and classy little house dating from around 1800. One of the oldest houses in the waterfront area, it was declared a national landmark in 1973.

The house stands in an area known as Peter Square. It was owned, and probably built, by Robert Peter, who owned a lot of land around Rock Creek and who became Georgetown's first mayor. (His son, Thomas, married Martha Washington's granddaughter and subsequently built Tudor Place with money from George Washington. But you knew this...)

Fast forward to 1951. Captain and Mrs. Rob Roy McGregor were looking for a Georgetown house with a river view. They proceeded to Memorial Bridge with a pair of binoculars to search the Georgetown skyline. One little house stood out, and when they went to look at it more closely, lo and behold, it was for sale! Now called the Brickyard Hill House, it had two bedrooms and four fireplaces, with original mantels and floors. The McGregors did extensive restoration, added a rose garden and installed big windows looking out over the river.

All these things pass into history. Or do they? Anthony Lanier, a visionary young Georgetowner responsible for many happy developments and transformations here of late — including the enormous incinerator project — had the little house moved across the street! Construction could be done underneath where it stood.

Now it has been moved back. It will become administrative offices of the Ritz Carlton Hotel now going up.

Things change, places endure, life goes on.

– December 2001

Down by the Riverside

SHELLS scoot. The river brims. A goose battles the current by Jack's Boathouse in the shadow of the great arches of Key Bridge. A two-person kayak goes by, the oars in unison, sleek and black like dorsal fins. This is our river, our splendid, noble river, finally to be showcased as it deserves.

Tucked along the river from Key Bridge to Rock Creek is a ten-acre parcel of choice waterfront that represents the final piece in a ninety-year-long project to protect the Potomac shoreline. For decades the Georgetown waterfront has been a profoundly unattractive industrial area, projecting grime and shabbiness. It just never was a good idea to use this prime land to park trash trucks and store road salt. Now, after long, at times well-intentioned, incredibly slow-moving, desultory, setback-laden progress toward doing the right thing, the right thing is about to happen.

Today's vision for a Georgetown Waterfront Park was first proposed at the turn of the century. In 1901, a plan for the Nation's Capital called for renovating our waterfront into a quay with adjacent public promenade and roadway. But nothing happened. In 1930, Congress recognized the importance of protecting both shorelines of the Potomac. Legislation called for federal acquisition and development of continuous riverfront parks. These parks were to be maintained and operated by the National Park Service.

Most of the land was transferred and protected, but not the historic Georgetown waterfront. It was the missing link in the necklace of greenspace along the Potomac. Not until 1967, and then only because it was included in the Georgetown Historic District, was it designated a National Historic Landmark, included in the National Register of Historic Places, protected by the National Preservation Act of 1966. But still no attention was paid to the waterfront per se, and still there was no greenspace.

Meanwhile, in 1949, the "temporary" Whitehurst Freeway was built, casting a perpetual gloom over K Street and effectively separating the waterfront from the rest of Georgetown. In 1980, the Washington Harbour complex was built on land owned by the CSX Railroad. Fortunately, a large hotel was not built east of Washington Harbour: that open space was saved by a downturn in the economy. Development of that land, however, may not be a dead issue.

In late 1996, the Georgetown Waterfront Commission was formed under the guidance of the Citizens Association of Georgetown. All interested parties were brought together to participate on the Commission. This was a citizens' initiative. Its goal was to work for the timely transfer of the land to the National Park Service, reach a consensus on the nature of the park to be created, and help find funding for its construction. It is believed that eight million dollars will be required to create the park. Senator Charles Percy chairs the Commission and Congress included a one million dollar appropriation for the park in the District's budget. This was a challenge grant, and $870,000 in matching funds have been raised so far.

The present day site of misuse and neglect will be transformed into a national public park with lawns, informal gardens, a fountain and waterside promenade. Adjacent to Key Bridge there will be boathouses for canoeing and rowing, as well as a waterfront restaurant. Pedestrian access to the east end of the park toward the Kennedy Center will be assured, a continuous bicycle path along the river will be created, and the tidelock at the confluence of Rock Creek and the Potomac River will be reconstructed.

The Georgetown Waterfront Park may not be quite ready by Fall 2001, the hoped-for completion date to coincide with the 250th anniversary of the founding of Georgetown. But the project is now moving ahead, and the transformation is going to happen. And that is very good news indeed.

– *May 2000*

Speaking of Bridges

THINK about it: in order to get to Georgetown from the south or the east you have to cross water, either a wide river or a small tumbling stream. Crossing water is full of portent and significance, and the bridges that carry us across are powerful symbols. Isn't everybody talking about bridges these days? Bridges speak the language of metaphor, are the stuff of legend and folk tales. Whether they carry us to the 21st century or only to Rosslyn, attention must be paid.

Key Bridge was completed in 1923. At its center it is 72 feet above the Potomac River. It has five great segmental arches and is a landmark against the Palisades trees, the Georgetown University spires and the Rosslyn skyline. It is beautiful.

The bridge was named for Francis Scott Key, whose house stood where the access road from M Street is now. According to Donald Myer's *Bridges and the City of Washington*, where much of this interesting material was gleaned, the traffic flow at the Georgetown end of the bridge was never well handled. Tell us about it.

Rock Creek and its bridges are a success story by every standard, respecting both the city plan and the idyllic nature of the tree-lined winding stream valley. We are the beneficiaries of good fortune and thoughtful planning.

Pennsylvania Avenue's bridge, low and serene, was built during the Civil War under the supervision of Montgomery Meigs of the War Department as part of the aqueduct system. Pipes underneath it both supported the bridge and carried water into Washington. The pipes are still there, visible today from the walkway below. The bridge had a wood floor, which needed to be replaced every three years, and it was too narrow to handle an increasing volume of trolley, wagon and foot traffic. The present bridge, built over and around the old one, was competed in 1916.

In 1800, President John Adams crossed Rock Creek on the K Street bridge to go to the new capital. Today this area is under construction, and a good thing, too. The many levels and uneven spans with ramps on both sides act as a barricade, obscuring rather than framing the place where Rock Creek joins the Potomac.

Just up river from Key Bridge the Aqueduct Bridge once stood. It was built to carry barges across the river, a concept that is difficult to get a handle on. Bridges full of water built to carry boats across water? The idea was to extend the C & O Canal to Alexandria without having to unload and reload cargo onto sailing ships, which would have been prohibitively expensive. The project, both bridge and canal on the Virginia side, was completed in 1843. The Aqueduct Bridge's life was long and difficult. Its obsolescence in the early 20th century resulted in the construction of Key Bridge.

Our bridges are beautiful and full of history, part of L'Enfant's grand plan. They lend awareness and drama to our lives. They fling us out of our little community and then draw us back in, and each one has a story. Even the ones that aren't there anymore.

– March 1997

The Handsome Row Houses of Georgetown

THERE are a number of series of beautiful row houses here in Georgetown, each row with its own stories to tell, each capturing a particular cultural climate or zeitgeist. But then, we have a long fertile past, and many zeitgeists.

On the east side we find the spectacular, ambitious and quite inspiring houses known as Cooke's Row. Eight first class dwellings on Q Street (3007 - 3029) with breaks in the numbering because of side yards. They were built between 1868 and 1873 as four twin villas by Henry David Cooke. Henry was the brother of Jay Cooke, whose Philadelphia banking house, Jay Cooke & Co., bankrolled the Union Army. Henry was a figure of personality and panache who first came here to run the Washington offices of Jay Cooke & Co. He and his wife Laura elected to live in modest, unpretentious Georgetown, even though the other fashionable people lived around Lafayette Square. He was a trendsetter, and for this we owe him a debt of gratitude.

With the election of Ulysses S. Grant as president in 1868, Cooke quickly became one of Washington's outstanding figures. In 1871, he became Governor of the Territory of the District of Columbia. Initially he lived at 1517 30th Street, now part of the building known as Downing & Vaux. Catty-corner from this house was an unimproved parcel of land which Cooke purchased in 1867. Upon returning from a trip to Europe the next year, he began planning his villas which were to include roof lines both French and Italianate — especially the pierced Mansard roof, the latest thing in Paris. The facades are picturesque, richly diverse, quirky and interesting.

25

In September 1873, Jay Cooke & Co. declared bankruptcy. Henry and Laura had to downsize and moved into 3007 Q, still unfinished. Henry Cooke, a vestryman of St. John's Church on O Street, had footed all the bills for Grace Church, built in 1866 near the canal. He died in 1881 at 56 and is buried at Oak Hill Cemetery amid 21 children and grandchildren.

Smith Row (3255 to 3267 N Street) forms a complete line of attached Federal-style houses stretching for an entire city block. General Walter Smith and his brother Clement picked up the vacant property between 1811 and 1813 and after the War of 1812 assembled the artisans to build the row of houses. Originally known as Knave's Disappointment, N Street soon housed a substantial merchant and business class that thrived in Georgetown in the early 19th century. Smith Row's houses are large and handsome with recessed panels between floors, fanlights, high dormer windows and pitched roofs. By 1872, N Street was on the schedule to be paved. An enormous sycamore planted in 1820 had its roots embedded in the dirt road in front of number 3265. According to Mary Mitchell's *Chronicles of Georgetown Life*, little boys would join hands around its 10-foot diameter and give it a hug. The tree stood more than 100 feet tall and took more than a month to remove.

Colonel John Cox, mayor of Georgetown from 1823 to 1845, built Cox Row (3331 to 3339 N Street) between 1815 and 1818. These grand imposing houses with their dignified facades, traceries and recessed festoons are excellent examples of Federal-style architecture. Colonel Cox who lived at 3339 N threw a party in 1824 for Lafayette in the vacant house next door at 3337. Lafayette, hero of the Revolution, arrived from Baltimore with a troop of cavalry and found a great banquet waiting for him there. The *piece de resistance* was an enormous pie made of 600 reedbirds, probably bobolinks. The Marquis is reported to have eaten a section containing 23 birds.

Another story tells how workmen constructing a fishpond found a tunnel leading to the river. What was it used for? Get away? Smuggling? Who knows? Bats flew out when it was opened and it was said that a small, pale man staggered out. A vivid imagination at work? Right now, three of the five houses that comprise Cox Row are having major work done. What might the workmen find?

– April 2002

26

Water Flowing Underground

DO you know why Reservoir Road is so named? It's not because of the present reservoir, where Reservoir Road meets MacArthur Boulevard. It's because our water supply used to be contained in a large structure where the Georgetown Library now stands. Have you noticed that the Library's iron fence along Wisconsin Avenue is ornamented with tridents, the emblem of Poseidon, aka Neptune, god of the sea? Of course you have.

In 1850, the population of Georgetown relied solely on springs, wells and rainwater cisterns for its water supply. These sources had become critically inadequate for drinking water as well as fire protection. Lieutenant Montgomery Meigs, a resourceful member of the Army Corps of Engineers, recommended construction of an aqueduct or conduit from the Potomac River above Great Falls to Georgetown. Accordingly, 14 miles of pipe were laid, through rocky hillsides and over a deep ravine at Cabin John, to three receiving and distributing reservoirs. These were Dalecarlia, the reservoir on MacArthur Boulevard, and the one at the present site of the library.

The water was brought in via large conduits under MacArthur Boulevard, which was known as Conduit Road. The pipes are still there. It flowed by gravity to M Street and Pennsylvania Avenue where it had to be pumped up to Wisconsin and R, the highest point in Georgetown. From there, good water pressure was assured for all of Georgetown

Captain Meigs then designed a unique circular domed building 120 feet in diameter and 50 feet high. In an effort to beautify it, the Corps of Engineers commissioned an elaborate cast iron cornice on the top of the dome. Six-foot high entwined dolphins surmounted it. They looked like the sea monsters you see on old maps, with big heads and puffy cheeks. Above them rose the trident standards, each with a gilded cartouche with the letters WA, for Washington Aqueduct, emblazoned on it. In 1932, it was torn down to make room for the Georgetown Library.

General (he kept getting promoted) Meigs' feat was remarkable. A 2000-man labor force completed various bridges and tunnels, and three reservoirs, in spite of a lack of funding by Congress, political intrigue and the disruption caused by the Civil War. The system was in full operation by 1865. In the middle of the 19th century, it was the most innovative water system in the United States.

It is still called the Washington Aqueduct system and is the private supplier for the District, Arlington County and Falls Church. As the system extended into Washington, think what it meant to the citizenry: the activation of public ornamental fountains and the beginning of the end for outhouses. No wonder the project was greeted with such widespread interest and enthusiasm.

Water — the source of life since we climbed up out of the primal ooze.

– February 2003

Cries and Whispers

SOBS and moans, muffled clanking as of chains being dragged, swishing as of ladies' voluminous skirts of long ago, ineradicable bloodstains, the pale face at the window, doors that open onto nothing. Someone has been standing in the garden, but no footprint is left in the damp earth. So how should one conduct oneself when former inhabitants drop by, even though they lived 200 years ago? October is a month of spectral activities; and we live in a town with a past.

John Smith noted 400 years ago in his diary a "moaning and sobbing" coming from the vicinity of the Three Sisters Rocks. Those are the rocks just upstream from Key Bridge, in case you didn't know. There is a legendary Indian curse upon them. It has to do with three Algonquin braves who were surprised while fishing and killed by an enemy scouting party. Three beautiful sisters who loved them determined to avenge their deaths and leapt into their canoe to do so, but the current proved too swift and the winds too strong. The sky darkened as they sank beneath the waves, but they had time to utter a curse: no one will ever cross the river at this point. In the morning after this ghastly event, there were three rocks where none had been before. And no one yet has crossed the river there — witness the failure of the Three Sisters Bridge project in 1972.

Even our bridges have ghosts: a drummer boy was blown off an early Georgetown wooden bridge and drowned. On still nights one can hear muffled drumbeats. Then there is the headless man of the K Street Bridge. He is beyond horrible, and no one who has encountered him will ever travel that way again. Francis Scott Key had a house that stood near the bridge that bears his name. In the years before it was torn down (alas), floors creaked when no one walked on them, doors flew open on rusty iron hinges and there were those bloodstains on the ceiling. Key was purportedly haunting later owners who had let his house run down.

Henry Foxall's house, which stood on 34th Street below the canal, had a "10 o'clock ritual." At that hour the house defied candles, gaslight and ultimately electricity. A "diaphanous aged woman" (thought to have once been the housekeeper) was to be seen floating through the third floor hallway. The house isn't there now, but is she still around?

Halcyon House at 34th and Prospect takes the cake for number and variety of hauntings. It was originally the home of Benjamin Stoddert, an early shipping magnate and first Secretary of the Navy. Toward the end of his life, sick, despondent and a virtual pauper, he would sit by an upstairs window with a spyglass, looking at the activity on the river. After he died, a widow living in the house preferred not to discuss the muffled sounds of slippered feet that she often heard from that room.

A carpenter working at Halcyon House at the turn of the 19th century heard tapping and rapping, moans and cries of despair, even blood-curdling screams. These were thought to emanate from a runaway slave who mistook the house for a stop on the underground railroad and was apprehended. A subsequent owner, the eccentric Albert Adsit Clemons, believed that as long as he continued to add on to his house he would not die. This would explain why he invited a carpenter to live in the house. Clemons had a lot of hang-ups. After he had the place converted into apartments, he made the renters change apartments every year so as to equalize the strain on the foundations. Apparently his tenants often experienced levitation and awoke floating above their beds (which must have temporarily eased the strain on the foundations). He buried two mummies in the garden, one representing his lost figure, the other his lost youth. It's possible Clemons had fallen victim to a vampire as he left instructions to have his heart pierced with a silver dagger after his death. And he actually did die, despite the best efforts of the carpenter.

We don't believe in ghosts anymore, do we? Certainly not just because it's October, when spirits are out and about. Wait, what's that noise? Who's out there? Turn the light back on! Aaargh.

– October 2000

Georgetown Above
and Below

THERE are thrushes singing each to each from the woods' edge in Dumbarton Oaks Park. They are more in evidence than they have been for years. There are house wrens in Georgetown back yards where they never were before, at least in recent memory. This probably doesn't mean anything — it may not be statistically significant — but in a time when the numbers of songbirds is declining, it is heartening nevertheless.

Two hundred years ago probably no one remarked on the shortage or abundance of thrushes and wrens. George Washington and Pierre L'Enfant were sitting down together at Suter's Tavern and figuring out how to create a capital city out of a malarial swamp. Now, of course, everyone wants to know where Suter's Tavern actually was. The site is buried somewhere, most likely near the intersection of Water and High Streets (roughly K Street and Wisconsin Avenue). The construction going on at the incinerator site there may yet reveal its location, but no luck so far.

Construction plays right into the hands of urban archaeologists. All those layers of earth, potentially chock-a-block with buried history. Federal law mandates that each construction site using federal funds must have the services of an archaeologist. This seems so sensible and, well, cultural, and provides us with objects and information that otherwise would be lost to the tender mercies of the bulldozers.

The two big projects in this area lately are the Whitehurst Freeway reconstruction and the incinerator site. Reports on these sites are not yet completed, but the freeway project has turned up many Native American findings and artifacts. Among the more interesting finds is what is believed to be a prehistoric ceremonial center with stone tools, hearths, necklaces of sharks' teeth, a stone phallus and an antler comb or headdress that flares out at the top. These treasures date from 750 to 1300 A.D.

In 1790, in the same general area as the ceremonial center, stood the house of Thomas Peter, son of Robert Peter, first mayor of Georgetown. Thomas Peter was married to the granddaughter of Martha Washington. (It was he who built Tudor Place.) Lots of artifacts turned up at that site: a black basalt bowl, glass, nails, ceramic pieces interesting not just in themselves, but because of what they tell us about domestic life in the early days.

The archaeologists involved in these projects are hoping to resuscitate the Washington Archaeological Society. This is a group of professionals and regular folks interested in our local archaeology.

We are, in fact, all archaeologists when digging in our own back yards. Recently, a neighbor noticed a shell midden exposed by the excavation for a garage near her house. Look at the sides of the excavation — that's where things turn up.

It's all about the relentless passage of time. Because we record ourselves so assiduously, curious people centuries from now may not have to reconstruct our lives from the frying pans, car parts and broken *tchotchkes* they find in the earth where Georgetown used to be.

The wrens and thrushes, how then will they fare? And will spring then be as beautiful as it has been this year?

– June 1999

Desire Under the Elms

THEY arrive like swallows. Suddenly they are everywhere, inspecting the places to make their nests (figuratively speaking), sitting congenially on the telephone wires, filling the trees. They are flocking here. Who are they? The people who want to live here. Everyone seems to want to live in Georgetown. This town has been around for a while, about 250 years, so why now?

Let's step back and look at this phenomenon. Does everyone want to move here, or does it just seem that way? Every block has a new young family that has just moved in. Where have they come from? Some come from far away, but many come from the suburbs, that former Mecca for young families. They are fleeing here, and they like what they find when they get here. No lawns, they sigh with pleasure. (But we do have lawns.) Realtors' open houses are social events as well as buying opportunities. They are beehives of activity.

Interviews have turned up the following insights. A family on P Street with two children and a dog has moved here from Bethesda. When a movie was being shot at their house in Bethesda, the filmmaker offered to put them up for a few months wherever they liked. They chose Georgetown, and of course they were enchanted. "There are no sidewalks in Bethesda, so it's difficult if not impossible to walk places. Here we walk everywhere. I walk the dog, my husband walks to the Metro. The parks are a great resource. The children play tennis in Montrose Park. It's more pleasant and lively; it's more fun than Bethesda. There is more here to engage the mind and spirit than sitting in traffic. The more time I spend not sitting in the car, the happier I am."

Another interviewee: "It's impossible to be lonely in Georgetown. There is a rich playground life, a rich dog life. You can walk to the corner market to get a loaf of bread. You don't proceed like a robot from your house to your car in the morning and then back again in the evening. Walking to the shops and the restaurants and encountering the abundant street life, you get to know your neighbors. It's a community." Ah, there's the word you hear again and again. There is no other place like it; it's a *community*.

Not only do people want to live in our houses, they want to look at them. That's why we have a successful house tour every spring. And strange as it may seem, *we* want to see how we live, because the houses on the tour are often, well, different from the ones we live in.

Tours of houses and gardens are such visual treats. Perhaps we are enchanted by the use of color, the abundance of light, a dancing fabric or a spectacular piece of furniture. "Caress the details," said Vladimir Nabokov.

A bit of vicariousness entertains us, too, as we see ourselves, ever so briefly, not in our known and predicable life, but in this other person's life. And we can be judgmental. We permit ourselves a *frisson* of pleasure at thinking we could have made such and such a room better, warmer, less stiff, and we don't actually have to do it, we can just think about it. People care about houses. They are the stage set for the theater of our lives.

On the east side of P Street, a recently redone house was bought and then boarded up all winter. Why? The new owners were redoing it yet again and replacing the glass in all the windows with old glass — more appropriate to the age of the house. Caress the details.

Markets tremble, but Georgetown houses flourish. Are we in Shangri-La, the great good place, the ideal refuge, the land of heart's desire? Not quite. But it's a very nice place to live. Ask the swallows.

– April 2001

34

Going On About Trees

THE British poet Gerard Manley Hopkins dearly loved the natural world and celebrated it in exuberant poems that were hymns of praise and joy. In "Pied Beauty" he wrote:

> Glory be to God for dappled things -
> For skies of couple-color as a brinded cow;
> For rosemoles all in stipple upon trout that swim...

But being a man of the cloth of that time and place, he decided he was enjoying himself too much. In order to be more humble and penitent, he resolved to cast his eyes only on the ground for the rest of his life.

Pity. He would have missed a lot of our Georgetown spring, had he lived here. Especially the trees. He would have missed the flowering of the saucer magnolias, the star magnolias, the Bradford pears and the weeping cherries. (We missed some of the show, too, because of the strange cold snap. The long border of saucer magnolias in front of Georgetown University Hospital was a sad sight after the frost.)

He would have missed the magnificent weeping cherry on the corner of 31st and P, to which we should all write poems. What about all our splendid American hollies and southern magnolias? On 34th above P Street there is a large and improbable Deodar cedar. For an exotic tree, notice the southeast corner of 31st and Q. That's a monkey puzzle tree. They're used a lot in England, but are uncommon around here. It's a science fiction sort of tree, different from the trees we're used to.

At Dumbarton Oaks there is a Chinese quince with a spectacular fluted, dappled, leopard-like trunk. There are the three stately and mysterious dawn redwoods rising from the interior of the block bounded by 30th, 31st, O and P Streets. Hopkins would have missed all this and the cryptomerias (Japanese Temple Cedars) clearly visible on O Street west of Wisconsin, and again on Reservoir Road just east of Wisconsin.

He would have noticed how our gnarled big old tree roots mess up the brick sidewalks in an attractive way — nature triumphant, nature prevailing over the hand of man.

Speaking of the English, in the 18th century it was chic to set aside a quarter of one's garden in which to be melancholy. To this end they created ruins, grottoes, torrents and barren rocky outcroppings and planted dead trees. As to dead trees, we have some 60 of them in our sidewalk tree boxes. No, they weren't planted dead. We are hopeful that the city will remove them so Trees for Georgetown can get on with their work. (Don't forget Trees for Georgetown, by the way, when you are writing checks.)

The *New York Times* reported that entire forests and ecological communities have migrated in response to major warmings and coolings of the earth's climate. Sugar maples, beeches, firs and spruces moved north as the world warmed after the last ice age. Hickories and oaks from the south moved up from further south. What's next? Our beautiful trees heading up I-95?

Now, in April, the next wave of flowering is upon us. Don't miss it.

– April 1998

The Volta Bureau:
"Mr. Watson, come here, I need you."

LOTS of things we don't know about go on in our community. What do you know about the Volta Bureau, the imposing Classical Revival-style building that stands on the corner of Volta Place and 35th Street?

The plaque on one side of the front door reads 'The Alexander Graham Bell Association for the Deaf.' On the other side a plaque reads 'Volta Bureau for the Increase and Diffusion of Knowledge Relating to the Deaf.'

Completed in 1893, the building was built by Bell to house his books and papers on deafness and hearing loss. Now the staff has just moved back in after completion of extensive renovations. The interior has been modernized and includes space for the display of artifacts and archival materials.

The place is now well-equipped to continue its mission, which is to help people cope with hearing loss. These days every newborn is tested for hearing loss before leaving the hospital. The Volta Bureau helps parents learn what they need to know to deal with an unexpected diagnosis. Funding comes from foundations, donations and more than 5,000 members worldwide.

Bell's interest was primarily in acoustics, which happened to lead to his invention of the telephone. He made it known, however, that he wanted to be remembered as a teacher of the deaf, not for his achievements as an inventor.

Although Bell was born in Edinburgh in 1847, his father moved the family to Canada for its more salubrious climate after Bell's two brothers died of tuberculosis. Later, Bell moved to Boston where he opened a school for teachers of the deaf. There he met and married Mabel Hubbard, who had become deaf from scarlet fever when she was four.

In 1878, he moved to Washington because of litigation related to getting the patent for the invention of the telephone. (There were men who claimed they had invented the telephone earlier.) Several lawsuits reached the Supreme Court, which upheld Bell's rights in all the cases.

Bell was an indefatigable inventor throughout his life. Other inventions he worked on included an electric probe for use in surgery (before the X-ray); a method of locating icebergs by detecting echoes from them; many experiments with flight, heavier than air machines, man-lifting kites; the hydrofoil; and always advances in acoustics and communication. He even tried to develop a strain of sheep that would bear more than one lamb at a time.

In case you wondered why it's called the Volta Bureau and the street Volta Place, it's because in 1880 the French government awarded Bell the Volta Prize of 80,000 francs, which he used to finance the building. Helen Keller was at the groundbreaking ceremony. The prize was named for Count Volta, an Italian, the inventor of the electric battery. The volt, a unit of electrical measurement, is named for him.

Directly across Volta Place from the Volta Bureau is the handsome house Bell lived in. There is a small building in back that he used as an office.

As for Mr. Watson, he was Bell's assistant and the first person to hear words actually transmitted via the telephone — words which were spoken by Bell because he had spilled battery acid all over his clothes.

Now you know.

– November 2001

Little Streets

PLACE, lane, court, row, terrace, close, crescent, dead end, alley, cul de sac, walk, mews, keys — call them whatever you like. They are charming little enclaves that add to the uniqueness and flavor of our community. They are so very Georgetown — quaint, stylish, intimate — but what do we know about them? What's their history?

Pomander Walk, Poplar Street, East Place, Suter's Lane, West Lane Keys, Dumbarton Rock Court, Orchard Lane, Avon Place, Cecil Place, we know quite a lot about them.

The passage of the Alley Dwelling Act in 1934 began the process that was to change the face of Georgetown and begin its transformation into the place we know today. The purpose of the Act was to clean up substandard housing. The first step toward this end was the razing of tenements. This process, and the dislocation that went along with it, proceeded sporadically in the ensuing years.

Then, in 1950, the Old Georgetown Act "to preserve and protect places of historic interest" was passed, effectively sealing the fate of those who had survived the earlier efforts at removal. The alley-dwelling families simply did not have the resources to undertake historic preservation. This was the new and final reason for the exodus of black families from neighborhoods they had lived in for generations.

But we need to go back a minute to 1934. Four small alley-like passageways were considered prime offenders for lack of sanitation, unsuitable standard of living and population density. These were East Place between 25th and 26th, P and Q; Poplar Place (now Poplar Street) between 27th and 28th, O and P; Bell's Court (now

Pomander Walk) between 33rd and 34th, P and Volta; and Cecil Place between Water and Grace Streets, on Potomac. Domestics had lived in Bell's Court for six decades, paying $12 or $15 a month in rent. It was a convenient location for their work at Georgetown University or in the big houses in the neighborhood. In the years after the passage of the Alley Dwelling Act, the residents of Bell's Court were served with eviction notices; the alley was deemed over-crowded and unfit for human habitation.

A resident of a nearby townhouse makes vivid the life of Bell's Court:

> "I have sat for hours on my porch looking at the alley and the big community backyard, opening off all the houses on the west side of the alley, and not even been noticed by my neighbors who are completely engrossed in singing, talking, fighting, washing, dressing, drinking, cooking, playing with the dogs and chickens or sleeping. On the first nice day of spring they put up a metal card table, and, as long as the rain doesn't exceed a slight drizzle, there are always four players sitting on boxes around it. Along the fence there are several chests of drawers from which half-clad figures frequently extract articles of clothing; there are two broken-down bedsteads; and there is a tumble-down outhouse used by the residents of this community in exclusive Georgetown when the crude indoor plumbing is out of whack — and that is very frequently."

The motives for displacing these people were mixed. In the 1930's and 40's, the influx of affluent whites coming in with the New Deal and then World War II created a Georgetown real estate boom. Substandard housing had been brought to the attention of civic leaders from time to time, but little had been done about it until the advent of restoration, which made these buildings attractive real estate investments. The improvement of living standards, yes, but the opportunity for developers to cash in didn't play an insignificant part in what went on. In fact, Bell's Court was not razed, but gentrified. From tenement to coach house: iron grill work over the entrance was to spell out the new name, chosen from an English novel — Pomander Walk. Like everything in Georgetown, our little streets have a history.

– May 1998

At Volta Park, Citizens Step In

AH, if this sweet old familiar, dilapidated, much used, soil-compacted, broken-concrete playground could talk.

For starters, it would tell you about more history than you ever imagined. In the 19th century when it was known as the Presbyterian Cemetery, some 2,700 people — soldiers (from the Revolutionary War, the War of 1812, and possibly the Civil War), ordinary parishioners and prominent citizens were buried there. Don't worry, they aren't there anymore, having been relocated around the turn of the century to Oak Hill and Arlington Cemeteries. (But in 1957 some boys playing in the park discovered a tombstone dated 1825.)

The departure of the departed left the area debris-strewn and in disarray. According to newspaper reports, some 50,000 bricks from a nine-foot wall surrounding the tombs were hauled away by private individuals for their own use elsewhere. Community action of an earlier sort.

Later, some of us remember when Jack Kennedy and his brothers played touch football there, and romance bloomed between the players and the young things who came to watch and cheer.

In recent times, Volta Park has had its supporters. Neighbors are forever having cleanup days, planting days, children's days. They care. Last spring when the District budget crisis resulted in the boarding up of the Recreation Center there, they watched with dismay as graffiti appeared and the park began to look not only neglected, but abandoned. An idea was then born which evolved into an organized and ambitious group, the Friends of Volta Park.

Under the able leadership of John Richardson, a much-respected contractor who lives nearby, a landscape design firm was hired to come up with a plan for the restoration of the Park.

The plan, now completed, includes flowering trees and shrubs, a watering system, new paving and fencing, regrading, re-seeding, new benches, seating for spectators by the baseball field, a picnic area, a pergola by the pool and flowering areas with perennials.

The Friends of Volta Park are talking about raising $200,000 to $250,000 from residents, businesses and foundations. The budget includes a 20 per cent per annum allocation for maintenance for five years. From the city, which is said to be very much for the project, the backers hope for mowing — and most importantly — a recreational director to run children's programs and keep things in order.

The District government already has an Adopt-a-Park program under the aegis of the Department of Parks and Recreation. Its objective is to form partnerships with neighborhood groups, with varying degrees of commitment on both sides. Thirty such programs already exist.

Volta Park's Friends see this project as a commitment to the future of Georgetown, and of the entire city, as 50 per cent of the users of the park are from outside Georgetown.

Like Bryant Park behind the main Public Library in New York City, which went from down at the heels and dangerous to a pretty good approximation of an English country garden, with a corresponding rise in morale, this project will be a touchstone for renewal.

There is no end to where it all could lead.

– October 1995

The End of Summer

SEA birds, farewell! Adieu beach pea, the breeze ruffling the dune grass, driftwood, the long summer dusk. Goodbye to the quiet mind. Sayonara bare feet and ice cream cones and the faint delicious sensation of something like irresponsibility — briefly felt, of course.

On the other hand, so long (thank heavens) to "Marco!...Polo!" which must have been repeated 1,000 times a day in every swimming pool in the country. By October we have achieved what the French call *la rentree*. They complete it in long lines of Citroens streaming in from the countryside — la France profonde — to the city. We just call it the end of summer.

The weather in Washington constantly confuses us, so we mark the beginning of real life by' a sudden dearth of parking spaces and a subtle change in the air that suggests that it's time to pull oneself together. Sigh.

Even if you didn't go away at all this summer, life changes at the beginning of fall. And if you did leave town, what did you find when you came back? Are we in Namibia, we asked ourselves? Is this the great red Australian desert? Burnt out grass, fissures in the baked soil. Drooping, suffering trees. And what about Rock Creek? It seems to be taking its name entirely too seriously and has turned into just rocks and no creek.

The only place you could find a thunderstorm was in the produce aisle at the Safeway. They have a creative little audio there that makes rumbling thundery noises just before they sprinkle the produce. No kidding. Right there by the lettuce and radishes. Special effects. Move over Steven Spielberg.

Who knows what's next climatically speaking? Probably hurricanes, probably not tsunamis, but you never know. Maybe a golden fall. It's whatever La Niña has planned for us. But the subtle simmering of the crickets only masks what we know is coming: bare trees, chill winds, early night. Maybe the answer is to throw ourselves into civic activities here in our little global village. Thus we could refute the prophet Jeremiah who said: The harvest is past, the summer is ended and we are not saved.

In any case, it is always worth reading again Robert Frost's lovely little elegiac poem, "Reluctance," which ends:

> Ah, when to the heart of man
> Was it ever less than a treason
> To go with the drift of things,
> To yield with a grace to reason,
> And bow and accept the end
> Of a love or a season?

– October 1998

The Vulnerable Among Us

IF we lived in an Edenic world, there would be no homeless. Or maybe we'd all be homeless, living in flowery meadows, lolling under fluffy trees, being fed on milk and honey, looking out for each other. Safe, we'd be safe there.

In big northern cities at the end of the second millennium, we are far from Eden, and homelessness is something else. The concerns are still the same: safety, getting enough to eat, and shelter. There are fewer homeless in Georgetown now than there were just a couple of years ago. This is due in part to a police crackdown — perhaps moving some homeless to other parts of the city — but the main reason is that the crack epidemic seems to have run its course. Crack is instantly addictive, a true destroyer of lives. One pursues it until one loses everything else and ends up on the street. Why is crack losing its allure? Possibly because younger people saw what it did to their elders and didn't like what they saw.

Drugs are still around, of course, as is alcohol, but the other major reason for homelessness is mental illness. When mental hospitals shut their doors, the mentally ill had nowhere to go but the streets. At that time, few monetary and medical resources were allocated for creating community-based services.

During the winter of 1984, an old man died of exposure on the streets of Georgetown. The Clergy Association heard about it and started providing shelter for the rapidly increasing number of homeless in our area. A committee was formed representing the churches and other organizations. In May 1988, the Georgetown Ministry Center was formed. Gunther Stern is the director, and the office is at Grace Episcopal Church on lower Wisconsin Avenue. Here the spirit of looking out for our fellow human beings is alive and well.

The homeless come in every day to discuss their problems with the staff and volunteers who are there to help them and put them in touch with agencies and services that can be of use. The Center also goes out into the streets to find homeless people. Always the continuing and underlying problem is how to make the system work — how to find permanent housing for them in a city with an unstable social service system, a financial crisis and red tape.

In the winter, the street people are taken in for the night at the various churches in Georgetown, on a rotating basis. They come in about seven in the evening, and cots are set up for them. Volunteers cook and serve them dinner. Unless there's bad weather, they leave about seven, after breakfast the next morning. For those people who don't want to come in, a Salvation Army truck goes around to provide a hearty soup and sandwiches. A psychiatrist works with the clients, both in the shelter and on the street.

Board members of the Georgetown Ministry Center are drawn from nine neighborhood churches, the Georgetown Synagogue, the Business & Professional Association, the Clergy Association and Georgetown University.

What can we do? Give money, donate food and clothing, volunteer. (Georgetown Ministry Center, Grace Church, 1041 Wisconsin Avenue.) Give to the social service agencies that try to effect real change, rather than to panhandlers as panhandlers are not necessarily homeless, and vice versa. Giving to them may just make you an enabler rather than a provider of real help.

Hundreds of people volunteer their help at the Ministry Center's various sites. Some of the names involved in this human drama, besides Gunther, are Caroline, Amy, Claire, Bob, Peggy, Beth, Breezy, Jeanette, Alex and Brenda. By their locations you may know them.

– March 1998

The Journey,
Not the Arrival, Matters

WINTER, the time to go for walks. Do you have any idea how many interesting walks, trails and paths there are right in, or immediately adjacent to, Georgetown?

The Capital Crescent Trail starts under the Whitehurst Freeway where K Street ends. It parallels the towpath for a while and then branches off toward Bethesda and Silver Spring. The Rails to Trails Conservancy converts old railroad rights-of-way into state-of-the-art trails. The Georgetown spur of the Baltimore and Ohio Railroad, later CSX, is now a paved trail with a grown-up yellow dotted line down the middle, kind of like a mini I-95. In this case, it's much more pleasant. The yellow line is there so that cyclists can avoid in-line skaters, who in turn can avoid walkers and joggers. There's a good smooth surface — you can go like the wind. The towpath has a perfectly good surface for walkers and joggers; the Capital Crescent Trail is state-of-the-art for wheels.

About the towpath itself, enough good things cannot be said. Parts of it do seem to be under construction a lot of the time, but that's because it's at the mercy of big storms. When it's beautiful, it really is beautiful. In autumn, the color blazes overhead and then — again — in the still water below. It is full of ducks and hawks and, in the spring, the gentle white haze of shadbush.

The towpath runs 184 miles through 74 locks to Cumberland, Maryland. That'll get you positioned to cross the Alleghenies, then the Great Plains and on to the coast. Westward the wagons.

The Glover-Archbold Trail crosses Reservoir Road just west of Georgetown University Hospital. If you go south after about a half-mile through pretty woods, you end up in a tunnel that takes you under M Street to the towpath. If you go north, it winds out toward the Maryland line, passing old stone ruins by little streams through more pretty woods. Excellent dog walking.

Of course there is the promenade along the river by Washington Harbour. A wide expanse of walkway gives onto the river. With a slight detour around the mouth of Rock Creek, you can continue on by the Kennedy Center and — still hugging the river — presto, you are at the monuments. Turning to come back to Georgetown opens up the view of Washington Harbour, which seems to evoke a medieval village. Roofs and towers and spires, and always the river.

From the back of Montrose Park a world unfolds. Proceeding down Lover's Lane, one comes upon Dumbarton Oaks Park with its lovely stream valley, a true jewel now being reclaimed after years of neglect. If you go the other way at the bottom of Lover's Lane, you are on paths that both follow and branch off from Rock Creek. These trails are well-marked with signs that give distance and destination, and even though you are in steep, beautiful beech woods, you are not lost. There is a network of trails; one can get almost anywhere. It is amazing. *Rus in urbe*. Countryside in the city. We have all this.

To put another spin on it, haven't all the great religions put an emphasis on a way or path? Walking is good for bones, heart and state of mind. The Romans knew this. *Solvitur ambulando*: It is solved by walking.

– January 1999

Rudist Colony

IT is a world of wonders. Georgetown has been repeatedly dug up and rebuilt and then built upon again. Layer succeeds layer until what we have is a kind of latter day Ephesus or Babylon or Ur. Not quite civilizations as in the land that lies between the Tigris and the Euphrates, but still history that is here for the digging.

For instance, excavation for the repair of the Whitehurst Freeway uncovered perhaps 50,000 artifacts, some dating back as far as 3000 B.C. — stone tools and ceramic pieces that are in a remarkable state of preservation. Out along the river, between Georgetown and Fletcher's Boathouse, there are very large storage pits that raise confounding questions about the ancient indigenous people who lived here. They seem to reflect the life of the native peoples from what is called the Middle Woodland period, who were here just after the beginning of the Christian Era, as we date it. But some cooking vessels and tools date back to 2500 B. C.

The colonists threw everything into cisterns. Today, that valuable colonial trash is prized by grave robbers, known as pot hunters, who loot archeological digs. The site of the Henry Foxall house (which around 1800, stood on 34th Street below where the C & O Canal is now) has produced old smoking pipes and wine flasks, 200-year-old Chinese export porcelain, European ceramics and Indian beads from the 17th century.

All this pales in comparison with what was found in a backyard on Prospect Street entwined in the roots of a very large black walnut. The workmen removing the tree unearthed several large (7 or 8 inches across) dense chunks of crystallized material interlaced with brightly colored tube-like structures. Red tubes, to be exact, in a milky white matrix. Amazing looking.

The owner of the tree had the presence of mind to go to the Smithsonian with her finds, where Mr. Raymond Rye, a paleobiologist, identified them as rudists. What are rudists, you ask? They are extinct clams that lived during the Cretaceous Period of geologic time. They and dinosaurs met their maker at about the same time, 65 million years ago. Rudists are of special significance because they lived like corals, forming large tropical reefs, in fact driving out the reef-building corals and assuming the dominant role in building tropical shallow-water reefs.

Here's the mysterious part: rudists are exotic to the bedrock of Georgetown. They never existed here alive. Therefore, suggests, Mr. Rye to the present owner, "They were either buried or discarded by some adventurer who preceded you. A likely source is the Middle East, possibly Israel." So speculation has focused on Albert Adsit Clemons, the unusual gentleman who lived in Halcyon House at 34th and Prospect in the 1920's. He collected all sorts of odd objects from world travels and is believed to have had numerous storage areas in the vicinity of his house.

Maybe there are rudists in the bottom of your garden. If you have turned up anything particularly old or curious in your backyard, please contact the Citizens Association. We are interested in placing ourselves on the time line here, whether it is in relation to the original inhabitants of the region or our more immediate Colonial forebears. Beyond that, receiving messages from creatures that lived 65 million years ago puts us rather effectively in our place.

What answers may come out of disturbed earth? Indeed, what questions?

– May 1999

Strutting Our Stuff

The 69th Annual
GEORGETOWN
GARDEN
TOUR

"Looking back, Georgetowners can see that it was in the late 60's and early 70's that the 'tourist trade' merchants and developers really fastened their grip on Georgetown. Glossy magazine articles touted stylish boutiques, quaint ambience and exotic restaurants. Soon Georgetown was known for its upscale shopping and benefit walking tours of the homes and gardens of the rich and famous."

Black Georgetown Remembered
Kathleen M. Lesko, Ed.

True, but actually both our house and garden tours have been around for more than 70 years. They're a continuum in a Georgetown that has, over time, presented many different faces to the world.

The decoration of life. The Greeks understood it. So did the Mings and the Medicis, and so did the Ottomans, Imperial Russia and Georgian England. It's about design, and design is about pleasing the eye. We ask not just does something work, but does it look right? No, better than right, does it look smashing?

Each spring, tour goers in Georgetown can answer these questions in their minds and imagine themselves in this kitchen or that living room, or having a quiet sit in those wonderful gardens. We can borrow ideas shamelessly. We can all be mini-Martha Stewarts.

Spring came early this year. All in a rush Georgetown had to think about getting back into showoff mode. We cast off our business-as-usual demeanor and morph into our role of coquette, seductress and siren as we have for years. Looking out from under our canopy of flowering trees, we bat our eyes at the world and say:

Come see us! We are something special! Have we got some treats for you!

This year the House Tour will be on the weekend of April 29th, with six houses open Saturday and six on Sunday. Some are interesting historically, some showcase interior design and some stand out for architecture. Treats will include an old farmhouse — done up, of course; a genuine Adams ceiling brought from England; a *tour de force* opening up of a southern wall with a garden view designed by architect Outerbridge Horsey; and the latest and best in professional interior design, reflecting a time of prosperity. In good times, there is a kind of flowering, with houses and gardens getting special attention.

A week later we move outside to the annual Garden Tour, this year for the first time being put on by the Georgetown Garden Club. Twelve gardens will be open to the public on Saturday, May 6, from 10:30 till 5 pm, rain or shine. More opportunities to be Martha Stewart.

Some highlights include a very stylish garden that combines serene European formality with American warmth; a small charming garden with gnarled crabapples, climbing roses and the patina of age; and a big garden — romantic beyond belief — with roses, trellises and doves' nests. Some are professionally designed; some are the work of their owners.

These tours enjoy a reputation, drawing admirers from faraway places. That's flattering, of course, and should encourage us locals to join in and visit houses and gardens we have always secretly wondered about.

– April 2000

Sheep May Safely Graze

Francis Scott Key House

MUCH ink has been expended on the subject of the demolition of the little house on O Street. Ink and outrage. So why do we care?

In the 1950's, sheep grazed in an orchard in the interior of the block bounded by 30th and 31st and P and Q Streets. At this time of year there were lambs in the buttercups. More recently, burros and mules adorned the hillside where the French Embassy and Hillandale are now.

Our little neighborhood has had many incarnations. Listen hard and you can hear the sounds from the commerce of the port town we were way back, the tobacco barrels rolling over the cobblestones. Then came the cries of the street vendors and the rattle of the delivery carts, and later, the trolleys.

There was the sound of marching feet heading south. Then for some decades Georgetown was a shabby little place. Around the turn of this century, and after World War I, things slowly began to turn around. In the 1930's and 1940's, the gathering troops of the New Deal, and then World War II, brought an infusion of people who helped fuel Georgetown's long renaissance from rundown country village to congenial residential area for the growing city next door.

In the 10 or 15 years after World War II, some among us recall Georgetown as a permanent floating cocktail party — presumably with some serious business mixed in. The guys lived in one group house; down the block the girls lived in another. Listen, you can almost hear the clink of ice in the glasses, the laughter in the streets.

Many incarnations.

We aren't a swampy little malaria-ridden town anymore, and we don't yearn to return to the days of the corset and the contaminated water supply, but we like our history, and we take it seriously. It's part of the tapestry of our lives, and it makes Georgetown an interesting and classy place to live.

The house at 3245 O Street dated from 1812. That's old. It was a worker's house. There is only one other house — in the 2900 block of O Street — remotely like it. To be sure, we have grand houses from even earlier — Tudor Place, Evermay, Mackall Square. But no small houses like 3245 O, set back from the street and free-standing, with its gable end turned toward the street. It was unique also because it was one of those houses, rare in Georgetown, that stand at the end of a street. You could see it from a great distance. Its counterpart, its bookend, is Dean & DeLuca at the old market. Now looking up Potomac Street from M Street, the visual impact is gone.

The Citizens Association is adamantly opposed to any further loss of our historic resources. But will what was allowed here — demolition as a consequence of neglect — set a precedent? We are an old neighborhood, and things will continue to deteriorate if they are not maintained.

Many incarnations, and we need them all. It's about context, diversity and layers of history.

– June 1997

To Please the Eye

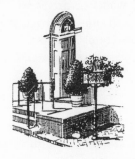

THAT clever, multi-talented fellow Oscar Wilde pronounced himself an aesthetician, by which he meant, one supposes, a producer and appreciator of things beautiful. It's a word we need here in Georgetown where we are favored with many aestheticians, both admirers and admirees. We fully value how things look; indeed we prize and cherish the appearance of things. That's what makes living here something out of the ordinary; there is much to please the eye.

The efforts of lots of people have made a difference, and one of the groups to which we should be most grateful is the Georgetown Garden Club. They go around seeing what needs to be done and then quietly do it. (Their role in the Volta Park restoration is considerable!) Recently they addressed themselves to our tree boxes — the rectangular planting beds at the base of sidewalk trees.

The Garden Club has produced a handsome brochure suggesting various treatments for these street tree-planting areas. The solutions offered are not only attractive, but have some chance of surviving, and even flourishing, despite the inconsiderate dog walker or litterer.

The club has recently given beautification awards — blue, red and green ribbons with handsome gold lettering — to the outstanding tree box plantings this year. On the day of the Georgetown Garden Tour, award ribbons were placed in the winning tree boxes. Winners didn't even know they were being judged, or that anyone was valuing their efforts. What the jury which made the selection was saying was "We have noticed what you have done, and we are grateful."

First prize went to 3259 N Street, a planting that definitely catches the eye as one walks or drives by. A border of beautifully maintained ivy rims tall and immaculate ferns. Flanking the entrance to the house are stately pots of columnar arborvitae underplanted with annuals. The effect is grand. It's classy. Think London, or Paris.

Second prize went to 3015 P Street. Handled in a completely different manner, the treatment here is cheerful, colorful and charming. Copious bright orange and white pansies mingle with variegated green and white plants. It's crisp and quite adorable.

Third prize went to 1505 35th Street. This solution is simply very tidy, with a low brick retaining wall and manicured ivy. It looks and is neat.

So this is what it's all about: a streetscape to be proud of Graceful curving iron railings, a slant of light across mellow old brick, tall French windows opening out under a canopy of trees, a fanlight, a filigree of demilune above a Federal doorway, planters that frame an entrance and echo the color and texture of the tidy tree box planting. It seems appropriate, civilized.

Appreciate us, these things seem to say. And we do, we do.

– June 1998

Daffodils and Dread

TO keep us from thinking about annihilation, let's change the subject, at least briefly. Let's see now, what's the farthest thing you can think of from death and destruction? It's gardens! Of course. They are good places to go to bind up the soul even if at this time of year we can only go to local gardens best by way of the bookshop.

Gardens have their handmaids, acolytes, priests and perpetrators. (Perpetrator doesn't necessarily mean a person who does something wrong; it means a performer, a doer.) In particular, two who loom large in our lives as perpetrators and interpreters are James van Sweden and Adrian Higgins.

Jim van Sweden has just published his fourth book, *Architecture in the Garden*. It joins *Gardening with Nature*, *Gardening with Water*, and *Bold Romantic Gardens* to make a significant contribution to our gardening bookshelves. It was van Sweden who brought grasses into our lives, massing plants in great waves to create abstract paintings on the land. His palette and his style are unmistakable, whether it be the sweep of tone and texture in the plantings by the State Department or his signature small gardens in Georgetown. Van Sweden and his partner, Wolfgang Oehme, pioneered a style known as the New American Garden. It has grown well beyond such a parochial description.

Adrian Higgins creates gardens, too, but we know him best as a glorious interpreter of what we see. He is a silver-tongued wordsmith. We see more fully because of him. As the garden writer for The *Washington Post* and as author of *The Secret Gardens of*

Georgetown, he never runs out of fresh ways to tell us what we need to know — and didn't even know we needed to know. Higgins is like a landscape painter. All those greens! How to describe them so you can really see them? Look more closely and you will notice other colors in the greens, nuances, subtleties, depths and distances. In gardens there are clouds and sunlight, water and arbors, steps and coping, niche and sill. Nature isn't all green anyway, but Adrian Higgins makes whatever aspect of gardening he is writing about fresh and evocative, every time.

In these murky times, we must concentrate on small pleasures. As Vladimir Nabokov said about gardens, we must notice and fondle the details. We must be the ones on whom nothing is lost. Hopefully, we will be doing this in just a month or two when on the hill at Dumbarton Oaks there will be cobalt pools of scilla and chionodoxa, rivers of forsythia and daffodils.

In the meantime while we're waiting for spring, think about the alchemy of pattern and design spelled out in lawn and paving, roses, hollyhocks and lavender. Blue Siberian iris like flights of butterflies. Creamier roses, darker pansies, and lilacs, which need no modifiers. Apple blossoms blowing across the garden like a plume. Radiant landscapes, the dripping shell on the mossy wall, the dancing bacchante, the collective memory of beauty and light.

Well, as the *New Yorker* used to say, no more vivid writing, please. So back to the message: Enjoy the moment! Here's Ezra Pound:

> Erat hora
> "Thank you whatever comes," and then she turned
> And, as the ray of sun on hanging flowers
> Fades when the wind hath lifted them aside,
> Went swiftly from me. Nay, whatever comes.
> One hour was sunlit and the most high gods
> May not make boast of any better thing
> Than to have watched that hour as it passed.

– March 2003

Asolare

IT isn't really summer in Georgetown until the town drains out and the air turns palpable and heavy like a wet towel. When the discomfort index hits whatever and the weatherman talks about code red in a portentous way, then it's getting to be summer. When the ground in front of the house looks like the Anvil of the Sun, the desert Lawrence of Arabia had to cross to get to Aqaba, and the shady garden in back gets each day more dank and spidery, then it is high summer. When the cicadas start singing and the cardinals stop, then and only then some of us start to bloom like an unexpected white clematis on a fence.

For some like it hot.

Then occur moments of pure summer bliss, with a breeze on the porch, books to read and time to read them. If a kindly neighbor gives access to a pool, and there is nobody there but the resident box turtle and a mockingbird, is this not close to heaven on earth? It is days like these Virginia Woolf was thinking of when she wrote, "One wants to say to the moment, 'Stay, you are so fair.' "

But as early as July mail starts to arrive demanding commitment in September. We should cry out that there hasn't been enough time for heat and dust, for idleness and reflection, for *asolare*.

Asolare, that's what it's all about. *Asolare*, the purposeless, leisurely, agreeable passing of time. The word comes from Italy, from the town of Asolo in the Veneto. Browning, who spent time in Asolo, thought the word was *asolando* and it meant to disport in open air or amuse oneself at random. You get the idea. Asolo has always been a place for writers, artists and "idle elegants." Think of crushed grapes, cypresses and wild thyme, the distant drone of bees, good conversation with clever friends.

Europeans are no doubt better at this kind of thing than driven, angst-ridden Americans. When the pace quickens in the fall, it's heady to take up our lives again after the summer, feeling important and useful and all that. But a small corner of the soul should accept only with reluctance the snares and fetters of September and beyond.

– September 1995

Rose Park Resurgent

IN the late afternoon, many small children rotate around Georgetown's playgrounds like heavenly bodies in the firmament, like traffic in a rush hour cloverleaf. Clusters of them converge and dissolve with regularity at the two playgrounds on the east side of Wisconsin, and a similar but different crowd meets at Volta Park. What tells them when and which playground? It must be synchronicity — the phenomenon whereby people and animals and birds all around the world suddenly do the same thing, although they couldn't know the others are doing it.

Rose Park definitely has its crowd, and in the late afternoon it is a scene of great felicity. Dear old Rose Park, a park with a history, a park with a future, a park for right now. It's got something for everybody. In the 1930's it was a focal point of black Georgetown, fostering tennis stars and fielding softball teams, putting on parades, pet shows and a summer camp. It was a true community center. When the Department of Recreation put up a "For Coloreds Only" sign in 1945, blacks and whites alike petitioned to have it removed.

Now it is having a face-lift, which Montrose and Volta have already had — and all indications are that it's a big success. It has been a labor of love for the neighborhood. Dog people, the above-mentioned little kids and their families, nannies, bike riders and hopscotch players, tennis, baseball and basketball players, seniors and singles have all come together to create and enjoy a multi-use park.

This has been an all-volunteer operation, a coalition of the willing, the neighborhood that made it happen. The Friends of Rose

Park have faced the constant challenge of working with both the National Park Service and the D.C. Department of Parks and Recreation, as both have jurisdiction. Happily, good relations have been built with both arms of the government.

The latest improvement is the tot lot, a dedicated space for the youngest visitors. Fresh new playground equipment has been installed, some of it right in the middle of the very large and inviting sand box. A structure rises from the sand, complete with pulleys to raise sand up to the highest level — rather like something that might have been used in the siege of a medieval castle. Other delights include a formidable wooden fire engine, little cars on springs, and climbing nets as are used in boot camp. The area is enclosed in a handsome new black iron fence that keeps the dogs out and the children in.

The Georgetown Garden Club is providing handsome plantings along the O and 27th Street approaches. Other improvements are to include a parking lot for strollers and baby carriages, four more benches, and new lights to be placed along the park path for safety.

Rose Park stretches from P Street down to M Street in a green corridor of grass, trees and activities. Inventiveness, imagination, aesthetics and hard work: How about a standing ovation for Rose Park resurgent!

– May 2003

Mrs. Bliss's Jewel

ENCHANT us, transport us, astonish us, we ask of art. Lift us out of our little routines. Take us by the hand to high civilizations. Remind us of forgotten beauty. Lead us into temples of the human spirit. Delight our eyes.

Over the holidays when the government shutdown darkened the museums downtown, art galleries like the Corcoran and the Phillips were able to attract and console disappointed tourists with their treasures. But the newspaper reported that the gemlike small museum at Dumbarton Oaks had no particular increase in visitors. "We are off the beaten track," a spokesperson said, "people don't know about us." Their loss.

The *tour de force* little museum designed by Philip Johnson to showcase the Robert Woods Bliss Collection of Pre-Columbian Art delights the eye indeed. Johnson's exquisite little round spaces — eight circles interconnect to form a square — surround a central circle where a jet of water dances out of a basin of gray slate set on edge. The domed circles have rich brown floors of wedge-shaped teak which taper toward the center. A ring of wide black marble surrounds each circle, and the light-filled domes are supported by fat columns of gray marble. The spaces sing, well, no, actually what they do is echo mysteriously.

Domes do that. The walls are all glass, giving onto a landscape of wet gray trunks, fallen oak leaves and snow. The out-of-doors is a presence inside the enchanting little domed rooms.

This is a building designed only as an interior, surrounded tightly by woods, not meant to be seen from the outside. A scholarly institution, it was not intended to be a "popular" museum and was intended for only a few visitors at a time. Reputed to be the most expensive building per square foot ever built, it is a supremely elegant setting for small objects. Said Philip Johnson of his client, "Mrs. Bliss had an eye... She was the perfect client, with a perfect program, with all the money in the world."

Then there are the objects themselves — a large porphyry rattlesnake, coiled and menacing, superb small jadeite statues from the Olmec culture and masks of fierce southern gods who gaze out unperturbed on these serene northern spaces.

This amazing jewel is right here, it's ours to be discovered over and over again. It's like a buried treasure, like a secret garden, like a clandestine love affair, the sweeter for the feeling that you, only you, are so favored.

The Dumbarton Oaks Collections are open daily from 2 to 5 p.m. except Mondays, national holidays, and Christmas Eve.

– February 1996

East Side, West Side, All Around Georgetown

SIDEWALKS, did somebody say sidewalks? Depending on how observant you are, how much you care and which block you live on, sidewalks are a hot issue. Who would have thought bricks could generate so much heat?

Feelings run high. We prize our street life. After all, it's why we live here instead of some sidewalk-less suburb with no soul, nobody around, and no place to go except in a car. We live in a neighborhood that has some "age on it," as they say with pride in the antiques business. We say it with pride, too. Old brick, that's important to a lot of people.

For the last several years, the city has been ripping up our old brick sidewalks and replacing them with new. Some of our neighbors wonder why it's necessary to replace mellow old brick that has nothing wrong with it with something new and out-of-place. Some residents have called up the Department of Public Works and, they say, have gotten it to relent.

But what about the other side of the argument? Old bricks deteriorate over time, tree roots push them up, holes develop and can become hazardous. Broken bones are no fun. And did you know that old brick retains water longer and is therefore more slippery when it rains, and much more slippery when it freezes? And the new brick the city is using is called "Georgetown," and its warm red color is really quite pleasing.

Today there are large patches where the sidewalks are concrete, and surely new bricks are an improvement over that. But that's not good enough for the purists. They are offended by the mismatched handicap access ramps at the corners of intersections; some are pink concrete, some beige. The city promises that all future ramps will be made of brick. It tries to be responsive.

What everyone should bear in mind is that 10 years ago, the plan was to make all sidewalks concrete. We dodged a bullet on that one, now didn't we?

Some things enrage the sidewalk purists, and should: litter purposefully dropped by passersby, half-full beer bottles propped in tree boxes, dog owners who commit the truly unpardonable offense of not cleaning up after their pets. At the risk of turning into scoop nazis, we should put out sandwich boards that read —

CLEAN UP AFTER YOUR PET
SURVEILLANCE CAMERAS IN PLACE

That'll get 'em. Or will it merely enrage those transgressors who will then redouble their efforts to bring their St. Bernards and Great Danes to our sidewalks every morning?

How to live, how to live? These are knotty issues. If you think you can just walk down the street oblivious to the details, you are wrong. They are the *mise en scene* of our lives. Would that our streets were filled with strolling players, jugglers with caps and bells, mimes, dancing bears, perhaps a *garde republicaine* on prancing horses, floats and festivals. We would move among them greeting our friends with nods and smiles. Would, too, that there were no longer cutpurses and footpads, now called muggers, running down our running bond sidewalks.

Look, we have these rosy rivers of brick flowing out in a tidy grid, bearing us where we want to go. We are swept along, nodding to our neighbors, hailing our friends and observing the passing parade. How fortunate we Georgetowners are, to "trip the light fantastic" on our sidewalks of old —and maybe some new — brick.

– February 1999

Flowering Georgetown

SLEEPERS awake! Remember sleet and freezing rain, our constant companions for so long? They have been routed, and now we are poised on the brink of the spring exuberances. Never mind about the mystique of the hidden gardens of Georgetown and the small paradises to be found behind high walls. If you know what to look for, a world of treats will reveal itself to the most casual walker of our newly refurbished sidewalks.

"Nature's first green is gold," wrote Robert Frost. And in early March, of course you noticed the strappy yellow flowers on the handsome pollarded witch hazels in the 2700 block of Dumbarton Avenue. They and winter jasmine, also yellow, are among the first bloomers, even earlier than the forsythia. Willows start out gold before they turn green.

Then all over the place appear lacy bursts of white from the star magnolias. Quince, with many small flowers of white, coral or red, changes from being a rather dreary shrub into something really quite showy. *Akebia quinata* (an assertive vine some regard as a nuisance) sports enchanting, delicate, chocolate-purple flowers which peek out from its handsome five-lobed leaves.

Hellebores bloom early and long in rosy pink, white and lime green. Shadblow (so called because it flowers when the shad are running), a native woodland bloomer, creates a haze of white in the woods along the canal and in Rock Creek Park. Of the glory and riot of spring bulbs enough good things cannot be said, nor about those who plant them out front where we all can enjoy them. Ah, we live in a bower.

Pay homage to the large drop-dead beautiful *Magnolia denudata* by the orangerie at Dumbarton Oaks. So spectacular is it that Mrs. Bliss (or was it Beatrix Farrand?) christened it "the bride." Another special effect nearby in that glorious place is just down the path to the right: a Chinese quince (*Cydonia sinensis*). A fairly large tree with lovely mottled bark, it has subtle soft pink blossoms in April or early May that you notice all of a sudden and feel somehow especially favored.

Cherry trees have achieved some prominence around here, and deservedly so. As usual, we will be lucky if the saucer magnolias are not zapped by a cold snap just when they are about to be at their most gorgeous.

In past years, the dense carpet of pansies — deep purple, maroon, orange, bright blue — in the tree boxes of the 3300 block of N Street have been spectacular. Try not to have an accident while driving by.

Which brings up the subject of tree boxes in general. Many blocks have gone to a good deal of thought and effort to make their tree boxes not only handsome, but relate to each other. In other words, they got together and improved their streetscapes. Pansies have gone in at 34th and P on the west side of Wisconsin, and stylish coordinated fences may be seen in the 3000 block of P. These neighborhood beautifiers deserve our undying thanks.

While we are cherishing the jewel-like pockets of flowers in Georgetown, the first green is washing over Rock Creek Park, our larger setting. Be sure to reread Louis Halle's superb book about it all, *Spring in Washington*. He says Rock Creek has the aura of dryads about it — a dryad being of course a wood nymph whose life is bound up with that of her tree.

– April 1994

Sleeping on the Hill

THERE is something strangely comforting about graveyards. The older they are the more comforting they seem. There lie all those people, safely dead these many years, with their mossy names and dates, perhaps their tumbledown stones, and their silence, which speaks to us nonetheless as part of the human narrative. "I had not thought death had undone so many," wrote Dante in *The Divine Comedy*. But of course that was disingenuous of him. He knew, we know.

Still, the comfort factor is real. Look at our local burying grounds, as they used to be called. Our most visible and most beautiful cemetery, Oak Hill, is a jewel of a park, maintained in perfect condition, set on a wooded hillside above a rushing stream. Vaults and obelisks, with carved angels hovering and Greek temples glimpsed, all gently infiltrated by winding paths beneath elemental oaks through glorious landscape. What a place to spend eternity.

In the 1840's and 50's, there was a movement in America to make graveyards less purely functional and more park-like. Mount Auburn Cemetery in Boston is an example. Oak Hill, established in 1849 by an Act of Congress, rode that same tide. The grounds are a major example of the 19th century Romantic Movement which advocated an acceptance of and blending with nature rather than a rigid imposition of forms upon it. The greatest proponent of the natural garden and its implication for cemeteries was Andrew Jackson Downing, and there is evidence, but no conclusive record, that he did Oak Hill's landscape design. James Renwick, Jr., architect of the Smithsonian Castle and the original Corcoran Gallery (now the Renwick), designed the iron enclosure and the Chapel.

Next to Oak Hill on the same hillside is a very different kind of cemetery with its own eloquent silences and mute witness. This is the cemetery for Mount Zion United Methodist Church, founded in 1816 and located at 1334 29th Street. Mount Zion Cemetery, which runs behind an apartment building in the 2500 block of Q Street, was originally two cemeteries: one the Old Methodist Burying Ground and the other for the Female Union Band. Oral history holds that the vault there was a stop on the Underground Railroad. We like to think it's true because it adds to the already powerful aura of the cemetery, which has recently been tidied up, gravestones righted, care obviously taken. The cemetery is a tangible reminder of the era when Georgetown had a large and vibrant African-American community. It's a haunting place and repays a visit.

How many times have we driven by Holy Rood Cemetery — on the hill above Wisconsin Avenue just north of 35th Street — and wondered just what its affiliation is, and who is buried there? It's the third cemetery of Holy Trinity Church and was established in 1932, probably in response to a cholera epidemic, after the church outgrew two previous locations. In 1942, Georgetown University inherited the cemetery in a realignment of church-owned properties. Not primarily in the graveyard business, the University has never seemed to be quite sure how to deal with it, and in fact the cemetery appears somewhat forlorn and neglected.

Which brings us to Volta Park, for many years the Presbyterian Burying Ground. Soldiers from the Revolutionary War, prominent citizens and ordinary parishioners alike were buried there, some 2,700 in all. But by mid-19th century it had become an eyesore, rundown and overgrown, with gravestones pillaged and vaults dismantled. Outraged families began moving their loved ones to other cemeteries. In 1891, crowds gathered to watch bodies being dug up. The abandoned graveyard was declared a park in 1907. Some 200 bodies were never accounted for.

Graveyards are tranquil pockets in a busy world. Think of them as the last frontier. They are places for reflection, and there is much to reflect on.

– March 2000

A Canal Runs Through It

BEFORE the dominance of the railroad and well before the invasion of the SUV — yes, there was such a time — America relied on water to move goods and people around. Where lakes and rivers didn't oblige, they built canals, creating a web of waterways into the heartland. So the Chesapeake and Ohio Canal was constructed from Georgetown to Cumberland, Maryland, beginning in 1828, and was intended to go through the Alleghenies all the way to the Ohio River basin. However, the arrival of the railroad effectively ended any hopes for commercial success, and in 1850, construction was halted.

The idea of a canal along the river wasn't a new one. Earlier, by 1799, men were working on making George Washington's dream of a navigable Potomac a reality. The construction of five canals around the river's impassable falls had begun. The bed of this early waterway, which proved unworkable, lies just under the bed of our present canal.

Although time passed the canal system by, the C & O Canal lives on. They didn't build it to enrich our lives, but it most certainly does. Ten minutes from home for anyone who lives in Georgetown there is a ribbon of quiet water fringed now with tall yellow iris and arrowhead; graced with geese and goslings. The grass is tall and feathery on the sides of the canal, and so are the trees. The city has disappeared. There are mallards and herons and turtles sunning themselves on logs, there are orioles in a big sycamore. When the dark water is still, it perfectly reflects the trees and clouds. There is a path along the canal that gives easy access to all this, and there are joggers, walkers, dogs and bicyclists who love it. As well they should. It is a treasure.

Our canal carries a lot of history, and sometimes it seems like we live in a stage set. In summer, and usually in late spring and early fall, the National Park Service's living history program produces men and women in period dress who work the mules and narrate the canal's history as the canalboat slides through the locks from Georgetown to Fletcher's Boathouse.

The Park Service representative for Georgetown for the C & O Canal National Historical Park works out of 1057 Thomas Jefferson Street. There, in a small house right by the canal, she monitors the goings on of our splendid little waterway. She looks out for the life of the canal. Urban and rural, past and present, its life is prodigious.

– June 2000

The Habitats of Volta Park

BY now we all know about the success story that is Volta Park — how a band of neighbors got together and formed the Friends of Volta Park with the intention of refurbishing the park, raised the money and just did it — ending up with a state of the art urban park with something for everyone. Have you been there? It has everything. It's like those pictures in children's books where every activity is happening in the space allotted to it.

At Volta Park the Little League is playing ball on the diamond, the parents are watching from the new benches, dogs are romping on the grass (with their owners cleaning up after them with the bags provided for that purpose), the tots are playing in the tot lot sandbox and swinging on the swings. Tricycle riders are wheeling away on the hard surface provided for them, and tennis players are competing in park-sponsored tournaments, with a plaque telling them about previous winners. Basketball hoop shooters are shooting, people are chatting it up at picnic tables, and a handsome new iron fence and stylish plantings surround all this.

What could this utopia possibly have lacked? Habitat gardens. And now there are two of them.

A habitat garden can be defined as an area organized specifically so particular plants, animals, insects and birds can interact with each other in a natural way. Those in Volta Park were made possible by the vision and perseverance of the Georgetown Garden Club. To implement their project, the members first raised money on their own and then applied to the Garden Club of America for its "Founder's Fund Award" which seeks to encourage projects like this one. They proceeded to win first prize in this nationwide contest, and that translated into a healthy boost to their funding, plus a lot of prestige.

There were two key points in the proposal submitted for the award: that there should be a strong interaction with the greater Washington community; and the importance of providing and maintaining habitats in urban areas.

Now, in the northeast corner of the park (the Q Street side) an inviting woodland path winds around a graceful berm bordered by native plants. Nearby, a sunny bank of flowering shrubs and perennials has been planted specifically to attract butterflies.

As this is an interpretive garden, there will to be signs letting visitors know what to look for, explaining the plantings and pointing out things of seasonal interest. This oasis in the city is designed as a teaching tool to show how felicitous a garden using native plants can be. The idea is to encourage others to do something similar, moving beyond geraniums, impatience and petunias, to discover how many other attractive plants there are.

Groups from local elementary schools will be encouraged to visit, and a guide from the Garden Club will be there to take them around. Children who routinely play in the park will be recruited to help plant bulbs this fall for bloom next spring.

To celebrate the opening of the habitats, a joyful ceremony took place on October 26th. Representatives of the Garden Club of America were there, as were people from the Department of Parks and Recreation. (After all, the city owns the park.) There were neighbors, a group from the Friends of Volta Park, and, of course, those members of the Georgetown Garden Club who played a significant role in making their vision a reality.

The community should give the Garden Club a trumpet fanfare and bang some cymbals. But not too loudly, please. We don't want to disturb any late season butterflies or bees.

– November 1998

The Very Rich Hours

MAKE your mind a blank. Let it travel freely in time and space. Picture a bunch of buildings clinging to the side of a hill beside a river. Steep cobblestone streets plunge down toward the river, and a bridge that looks for all the world like a Roman aqueduct spans it. The street life is diverse, animated, colorful. There are mendicants, fortune tellers, street musicians and merchants hawking a variety of wares. Knots of students cluster on street corners discussing the meaning of meaning or the latest heresies. Over all tower the spires of a great Gothic university. It is the 13th century, and you are in Heidelberg, or Bologna or Paris.

Wrong. It is almost the 21st century, and you are in Georgetown. You guessed it, didn't you?

But do you know about the riches our very own university makes available to the intellectually curious and alive? For some of us who have just discovered and partaken of Georgetown's continuing education program it came as a revelation and bolt from the blue that so many goodies were offered so nearby, for such reasonable prices, at convenient times, and there is a parking lot.

There are non-credit courses and credit courses and courses to audit. The catalog is over 100 pages long and just chock-a-block with succulent offerings: languages, law and public policy, creative writing, calligraphy, conflict resolution, personal finance, the cello, photography, screenwriting, ancient Rome, public speaking, the Richelieu wing of the Louvre, computer skills, oriental carpets, philosophy, women writers, the Irish theater, on and on. Whew! And *hermeneutics*. Do we even know what hermeneutics is, or are?

This list only skims the surface. When you walk by the open doors of the other classrooms on the way to yours, it takes an act of will not to linger, just out of sight, and listen to the lecture or the discussion.

Classes are offered in the evenings and on Saturdays in three terms a year — fall, spring and summer. Some courses are long, and some are short. Many are challenging. Most are mind-expanding. All are life-enhancing. They are full of interesting people; well, after all, this is Washington.

There used to be a poster that advertised the New School, another hotbed of learning. It featured the tin woodsman, the cowardly lion, and the scarecrow up in a balloon high above New York City. The caption read: "For a heart, courage or a brain."

Exactly.

– March 1996

The Old Becomes New Again

TEAR yourself away for a minute, if you can, from the seasonable exuberances — the wanton excesses — of spring in Georgetown. There's nothing wrong with looking at life through a veil of flowering trees, of course. But consider for a minute instead our built environment. A Georgetown landmark, our Post Office, is about to be restored. If all goes as planned, we can say goodbye to linoleum and formica and prepare to enjoy the noble vision of its original architect.

Here's what we know about its building in 1857 and what's now going on:

In the 1850's the federal government realized — after the Gold Rush — that there was going to be more to this country than just the northeast. If we needed post offices in the east, we would need them in the midwest and the west, too. So an architect from Vermont, Amni Burnham Jones, was engaged to build a prototype post office which could be easily replicated all over the country. For this prototype — our post office — he specified tall columns of cast iron with leafy Corinthian capitals that could be cast here and then taken west. The columns were linked by wrought iron beams that spanned a vaulted brick ceiling. The effect was a lofty space, open and attractive, and it will be again.

The second floor was a customs office until the 1960's. Heat for the building was provided by 12 fireplaces. The original floors were made of hard pine, and it's hoped that they can be replaced with the same. Hard pine, very difficult to come by now, is found only on river bottom land, mostly in Georgia. The foyer was, and may be again, of black and white marble tiles.

The plaza in front of the building is to be granite, with planters, and the fence will be like the original, somewhat more elaborate than the present fence.

All post offices are not restored with this much attention to detail and precedent. In our case, the support of D.C Postmaster David Clark made such flexibility and historical fidelity a possibility, arguing that it is undeniably a historically important building. Sorg and Associates, a Washington firm with a record in historic preservation, has designed the new building. Our own John Lintner, supervisor of the Georgetown Station, provided the historical context.

Here in Georgetown the character of our streets is enhanced by the interjection of a monumental building every so often, as our resident architect, Hugh Jacobsen, has pointed out. And all is enhanced by an aware and appreciative populace.

– May 1997

The Decoration of Houses

IN addition to her better known books, Edith Wharton, that redoubtable arbiter of taste and manners, wrote, with Ogden Codman, Jr., an informative little book called *The Decoration of Houses*. In it she speaks as from on high on matters pertaining to style, suitability and the avoidance of — shudder at the thought — vulgarity. Her book is both very dated and not at all dated, and therein lies its charm.

The word "decorating" has fallen out of favor these days. Everything is designed now, and thus we have food designers, hair designers and interior designers. This new terminology is designed (sorry) to make whatever it is seem more important. Mrs. Wharton would have seen right through such a ruse. However, even though she calls it decorating, it is also design that interests her: the placement of things, the interplay between masses and voids. She sees it as the counterpoint to architecture, and here are some of her pronouncements:

Proportion is the good breeding of architecture. The better the house, the less need there is for curtains.

A multiplicity of colors produces the same effect as a number of voices talking at the same time. The voices may not be discordant, but continuous chatter is fatiguing in the the long run.

There are but two ways of dealing with a room that is fundamentally ugly: one is to accept it, and the other is courageously to correct its ugliness. Halfway remedies are a waste of money

Do not acquire *parlor suits*. Do not be taken in by articles with hints for *artistic interiors* or the use of poetic adjectives such as *jonquil yellow*, *shell pink*. or *ashes of roses*. The arrangement suggested are usually cheap devices based upon the mistaken idea that defects in structure or design may be remedied by an overlay of color ornament. The result is never satisfactory to the fastidious.

All good architecture and good decoration must be based on rhythm and logic.

Well, we are leading up to something here, and it is the Georgetown House Tour, an enjoyable spring ritual that benefits St. John's Church. There are many who find looking at other people's houses fascinating, and rightly so. The visual impact of a bright, inviting room opening onto a pretty garden cannot be overestimated. Whether the interiors are to one's taste or not, there are always ideas and inspiration to be found. In the larger sense, of course, it is not just the houses themselves that engage us, but the quality of life in them as we imagine it to be — the classical question of how to live.

– April 1995

The Once and Future Park

GARDENS do not very often survive the gardener. But who any longer wants catalogues of ruin and loss, who any longer studies the sadness of lost gardens? Can we bear one more story of abandonment and destruction, of beauty vanished? "Many ingenious, lovely things are gone," wrote William Butler Yeats, summing up all our dread. But wait, an organization called the Garden Conservancy cares about lost gardens and we, the citizens of Georgetown, give every indication of caring about gentle amenities and life-enhancing places. So, while this is a story of loss, it also, just possibly, is a story of rebirth.

Dumbarton Oaks Park is a wooded retreat nestled on 27 acres below the celebrated gardens of Dumbarton Oaks. A winding stream valley there was transformed into a romantic setting by Beatrix Farrand, a towering figure in American landscape design. In 1921, Mildred and Robert Woods Bliss began working with Farrand on a plan for their new property that would include both the gardens and the larger parkland in a unified composition. In the valley, Farrand enhanced the stream with waterfalls, pools, stone bridges, a grotto and a waterwheel. Other picturesque elements included an arbor, meadows crisscrossed by a bridle trail and the use of native plants. The result was a resplendent landscape and, indeed, Farrand felt Dumbarton Oaks to be her "most deeply felt" work. All of which is a long-winded way of saying we have something special here, and attention must be paid.

In 1940, only seven years after the completion of the gardens and Park, the Blisses gave Dumbarton Oaks to Harvard University and the Park to the National Park Service. Farrand and the Blisses spent the next two years trying to assure that the Park Service would maintain the area as it had been maintained previously. Optimistic to begin with, the Park Service all too soon encountered problems: insufficient funds and siltation caused by nearby construction.

In 1972, Dumbarton Oaks Park slid into its present unfortunate state when the administrative structure for the park was drastically reordered and personnel familiar with it were retired or transferred. By 1976 when Dumbarton Park was returned to the jurisdiction of Rock Creek Park, unwanted growth was out of control, and the dumping of fill on adjacent properties had washed huge quantities of silt into the stream, damaging dams, ponds and plants. Neglect and uncontrolled storm drainage remain major problems. It's the familiar sorry tale of the cutting of promised funds, altered priorities, red tape and the loss of institutional memory.

Enter a citizen's group, the Friends of Montrose and Dumbarton Oaks Park, formed in 1992. It has already done cleanup and stabilization around the stream and has enlisted the support of the Garden Conservancy, which has agreed to help in an advisory capacity. Volunteers from the Harvard Club, the staff of Dumbarton Oaks, neighbors and other concerned citizens have cleared away the scrub and vines and reclaimed paths and meadows, revealing drifts of daffodils. Garden Clubs and other friends have donated money. But the built elements, the stream bed and the plants remain in a sorry state, awaiting a master plan.

The Friends group is initiating a Cultural Landscape Report, a necessary first step which will address underlying site and civil engineering problems. The next step will be to identify specific projects and go about raising funds, focusing on restoration and endowment. There is something abroad in the land now that responds to this kind of challenge; look at the response to the Volta Park project. Citizen groups working with the National Park Service have restored other areas. No one expects that the stream valley will look the way it did in 1940, but the decay and deterioration can be reversed. Hopes are buoyed by its national significance and its special status as an important work of the legendary Beatrix Farrand.

– April 1996

Le Sacre Du Printemps

THE time for rhapsodizing is upon us again, and not a minute too soon. Time, one hopes, to do again all the things we have done before, to observe exactly the same rites of spring this year as last. And then again next year, and the year after that. As Milan Kundera, that inscrutable Czech writer tells us, "Happiness is the longing for repetition."

Our spring observances — the daffodils on the steep bank above Rock Creek Parkway as it curves around P Street; the dazzling abundance of small spring bulbs in shades of blue, lavender and purple dotted with white on the hillside at Dumbarton Oaks; the clouds of saucer magnolias on Reservoir Road by the hospital; the carpet of Spring Beauties that flow between the tombstones at Oak Hill Cemetery. We who are still above ground are delighted to partake of this great feast of form and color and texture. These things must be celebrated. The surreptitious return of the catbird — one day it's back, a trim gray bird hopping out of the bushes onto the smooth gray flagstones. This is a sacrament of spring. And so, too, is the return of the wrens to Tudor Place.

People have their spring rituals, too. Here in Georgetown, we give tours —a house tour and a garden tour — and invite ourselves and others to admire us. There is much to admire. Our house tour is not just any house tour; it is America's first and oldest. This year, to gild the lily, we can see six houses by the master, Hugh Newell Jacobsen, named one of the ten most important architects of this century. We have the single largest collection of his houses. Why? Because he lives here, of course. His sleek contemporary facades integrate perfectly with our 18th and 19th century architecture, adding rhythm and style to our graceful streetscapes.

Last year, we inaugurated a new spring ritual. The Georgetown Garden Club, a quiet, efficient beautifier of our village, sponsored a competition for the most beautiful tree boxes. After all, a community is only as beautiful as the face it shows to the world. All the glorious secret gardens imaginable won't do a thing for the streetscape. Well-kept streets, trees and tree boxes make an enormous difference in the appearance of a community. Accordingly, this year the Garden Club is distributing a brochure which provides suggestions for suitable plants and edging materials and includes a useful list of resources. It is also sponsoring a free workshop with experts offering advice on designing, planting and maintaining tree boxes.

This is tricky and challenging. While it's relatively easy to create a beautiful tree box for a day or two, it's something else again to create one that will endure for a season. There are enemies out there: late night revelers and their discarded bottles and cans, other evil litterers, bad drivers who mistake the sidewalk for the street, wind and (shudder) most to be feared of all, dogs. Dogs. That's why edging or fencing is a must!

Street beautification is a serious idea and a good one. It won't hurt any of us to make a little effort for the common good. That's why we live here, isn't it? And if this means doing some maintenance to make sure the boxes stay looking nice, that's all right, too. The volunteers at that marvelous organization, Trees for Georgetown, work hard to make sure the street trees are kept looking nice and are replaced when they die. If they can make that effort, surely we can underplant them attractively. So come to the workshop, spruce up your sidewalk, enjoy the spring. Remember A. E. Houseman:

> And since to look at things in bloom,
> Fifty springs are little room,
> About the woodlands I will go
> To see the cherry hung with snow.

– April 1999

Landscape As Metaphor

IT is clever to say that landscape is a noun and garden is a verb, but in speaking of world-famous Dumbarton Oaks' landscape and garden, adjectives are needed. We neighbors care about that place because it is, well, beautiful. Elegant, graceful, formal, naturalistic, worldly, intimate, rich in detail, a provider of enchantment, a restorer of the soul, a national treasure, our treasure.

In 1921, Mildred and Robert Woods Bliss asked Beatrix Jones Farrand to make a garden for them. A major figure in landscape design, Farrand was one of eleven founders of the American Society of Landscape Architects and the only woman. At Dumbarton Oaks she combined formal and informal garden elements in a tiered composition that radiates out from the house and down the hill. She drew on the vocabulary of the great Italian Renaissance villas and blended these effects with the subtlety and color of the English flower garden tradition. The result was, and is, a resplendent landscape.

Since 1940, Dumbarton Oaks has been owned by Harvard University and is also a scholarly research institution. Having outgrown its present facility, it proposes to build a two-story underground library beneath the North Vista — the broad sweep of lawn with the grassy steps that extends like the prow of a ship out toward Dumbarton Oaks Park. To make way for the library, the stone walls and some of the landscaped beauty would have to go — at least temporarily.

Harvard has promised, post-construction, to restore the North Vista exactly as it is. Once the big holes have been duly dug and filled in, once the heavy equipment has gone, once the soil and grass and plants have been returned and the walls faithfully numbered, stored and restored, they say it will look just as it does now. Harvard has been a good custodian, so why should we question it now?

All very well, but this has provoked cries of outrage and pain from landscape architects who contend that no one, not even Harvard, should mess with an icon. Like all landscape art, it is extremely vulnerable. They argue that not enough study has been done, that Harvard's own resources in landscape design studies have not been used, that nothing can really guarantee that problems won't occur down the road. Most importantly, they feel that this is sacred ground.

There is an alternative site for the new library say the critics, by the Jelleff Boys & Girls Club. Far less desirable, says Harvard, for the proposed underground addition would enable the fellows (scholars) to have all the valuable resources and their offices in one place. If a new building went up, the present underground library, beneath parts of the Music Room and the Pre-Columbian Museum, would become wasted space.

All this is moving through channels and navigating the watch-dog institutions that guard our cultural heritage. Who knows what the ending will be? If the controversy raises our consciousness about Dumbarton Oaks, if it sends a few more of us up there next spring to be dumbstruck by the blue carpet of spring bulbs and the clouds of cherry blossoms, something good will have come of it. That's what being alive is all about.

Speaking to Harvard about Dumbarton Oaks, Robin Karson of the Library of American Landscape History remarked: "The spirit of the landscape under your care is extraordinary in its capacity to inspire ideas, emotions and undertakings that add to the general well-being of mankind."

You see, it's about more than grass and trees in a pleasing arrangement. But everyone is fully aware of that.

– December 1999

More About Georgetown's Bridges

THERE were fords across Rock Creek at M and P Streets in colonial times. Fords seem so incredibly romantic and inconvenient. In fact, the M Street ford was usable only at low tide and in good weather, so in 1788 a wooden drawbridge was installed. During a fierce storm it collapsed, plunging a coach and four into the swollen stream, drowning all.

The design of the present bridge was originally rejected as out of keeping with the other arched park bridges such as the Taft Bridge on Connecticut Avenue and the Dumbarton Bridge on Q Street. Nevertheless it was completed in 1929. Non-conforming or not, it is a handsome concrete-covered steel structure with pedestrian walks cantilevered out from the sides.

The stone arched bridge that carries P Street over Rock Creek was completed in 1935 and stands on an important historic site. It was a favorite fording place until the mid-19th century, and it was here that the Baltimore Light Dragoons and the French units led by Lafayette, Count Rochambeau and the Duc de Lauzan crossed Rock Creek during the Revolutionary War.

The P Street Bridge is quite plain, with a very low relief stone trim. It's in harmony with efforts to provide Rock Creek with individually designed masonry arched crossings and is a good foil to its elaborate neighbor to the north, Dumbarton Bridge.

Better known to its admirers as the Buffalo Bridge, Dumbarton Bridge is covered with a profusion of romantic sculpture and detail. It has a European flair executed with purely American themes. Georgetowners had originally considered getting a used bridge for the site, but ultimately decided they needed something of high quality and superb design.

They got it. Five large semicircular arches are crowned with smaller cantilevered brackets that cast deep shadows. Below the brackets are a row of sculptured Indian heads in full headdress, all made from a life mask of Chief Kicking Bear. They are indeed impressive seen from Rock Creek Parkway below. The bison on top of the bridge are immensely noble and should remind us every day of who we are and where we as a country came from. Both the Indians and the bison are the work of sculptor A. Phimister Proctor.

In the early 19th century, a charming series of bridges crossed the city's canal system. Of these only the Wisconsin Avenue Bridge remains, just as the C & O Canal is the only part of the canal system that remains. Today automobile bridges cross the canal at 29th, 30th, 31st and Thomas Jefferson Streets, and there are pedestrian bridges at 33rd and 34th Streets. These small bridges are the only remaining vestiges of the city's early canal and bridge transportation.

History lives. When you enter Georgetown on M Street, remember you are being carried over the stream on a haunted, archless bridge. When you come in by P Street think of the Marquis, the Count, and the Duke, the water up to their stirrups. At Dumbarton Bridge, reflect on our country's vivid origins. And never for one minute think we live in a drab little place with no stories and no past.

Note: Most of this interesting information comes from *Bridges and the City of Washington* by Donald Beekman Myer. If you want more, that's where to find it.

– April 1997

And Now, Book Hill

WHAT becomes a community most? The appearance of its streets and buildings, the gracefulness of its public spaces, and the enterprise and goodwill of its citizenry. So it's time to give us citizenry a little pat on the back. We have been doing very well. Everywhere you look, in everything you read, people are volunteering, donating, pitching in, beautifying, enhancing, celebrating.

Is this our golden age? Perhaps. By our works you shall know us. Trees for Georgetown is a citizen-driven effort that plants and maintains the trees on our residential streets. The restoration of Volta Park is a model for parks all over the city. Rose Park is coming along well under the aegis of the Friends of Rose Park, which has the challenging job of working with both the District of Columbia and the National Park Service. Montrose and Dumbarton Oaks Parks recently celebrated the strides that have been made in restoration initiated by citizen impetus and involvement.

Now Book Hill, that pleasant little hillside that floats down toward Reservoir Road and Wisconsin Avenue from the commanding heights of the Georgetown Library, is benefitting from the attention of the community. Run down and neglected for years, it is enjoying a rebirth because a group of neighbors formed the Friends of Book Hill and went to work.

They started out trying to do the work themselves, found it too much for them and hired a professional arborist and a professional landscaper — both of whom donated a percentage of their fees. They cleared out the messy woods where the homeless camped, pruned the raggedy overgrown vines, and removed the dead trees and general debris. Next they will re-space the azaleas that border the long agreeable flight of steps, then add new shrubs and blooming perennials. They were aided in this effort by a small grant from Garden Resources of Washington (GROW), a foundation that promotes organic gardening and community participation.

A croquet tournament and raffle on the lawn were planned for the day of Georgetown's 250th Anniversary Parade, but the event was rained out. Not the parade — which definitely was not rained out. The parade was, in fact, a huge, stirring, completely wonderful event that captured the enduring style and indomitable spirit of Georgetown. Never better! What a parade! What a splendid community!

So this winds up a very good year for Georgetown. Look how much fun we have had. And it's June, beautiful June, with all these inviting outdoor places to enjoy. Remember what Edith Wharton said were the most beautiful words in the English language: *summer afternoon.*

– June 2001

Scents and Sensibility
Remembering Christmas Past

THERE is always more to the season than meets the senses. More than this year's wrapping paper and fruitcake, more to it than the silver bells and mistletoe.

There are all those other Christmases. Such a time for dredging up the past. Think of all that emotional baggage we handcarry through life or which lies checked in the baggage room of our minds, waiting to be stirred to life by a word, an object or a faint familiar scent, calling up those old pleasures and dreads. There they are, those eggnog parties and faces around the piano, those car trips and family reunions of long ago. Other voices, other rooms. Lost magic. Houses we will not enter again, cheeks we will not kiss. All, all there.

Deep in our brains lie two little structures, the amygdala and the hippocampus. Vital to the formation of long-term memory, they deal with emotion — and emotions play a major role in what we remember. Part of what is called the limbic system, they depend on an intricate network of sensory connections and are closely related to the olfactory system. All of our senses evoke memory, but none more strongly than smell and taste (and taste is a derivative of smell).

Thus smell + emotions = memory. How unromantic! Our powerful and splendid memories seem so sterile when described like this. And smell? Really. Who talks about smell anymore anyway? It's fragrance.

The fragrance of the florist's shop with its steamy winter windows and the aura of the warm South. Or perfume. It can transport us instantly to a world of satin sheets and breakfast trays on the veranda. The whiff of a certain pipe tobacco and a whole lost world springs up before us.

Proust knew how taste and smell evoke memory. Consider the famous passage about the madeleine from *Remembrance of Things Past*: "My mother, seeing that I was cold, offered me some tea. And soon, mechanically, weary after a dull day with the prospect of a depressing morrow, I raised to my lips a spoonful of the tea in which I had soaked a morsel of the cake. No sooner had the warm liquid, and the crumbs with it, touched my palette than a shudder ran through my whole body... An exquisite pleasure had invaded my senses...Suddenly the memory returns...the whole of Combray and its surroundings, taking their proper shapes and growing solid, sprang into being, town and gardens alike, from my cup of tea."

So it is with this holiday season. The pungent odor of pine, the aroma of roasting turkey, the bouquet of wine, fruity punch, sweet-scented packages, thoughts of frankincense and myrrh...balm of Gilead, attar of roses, tinctures and oils, and on and on. By all things spicy, musky and flowery we will be borne back into the past.

If we aren't too exhausted. And if we are, well, there is always aromatherapy.

– December 1996

Odd Thoughts at the Year's Turning

THE end of one year and the fresh slate of a new one tend to elicit vague, disquieting thoughts of mortality. We are reminded that life is a fragile and uncertain enterprise. All those summings up, all those new beginnings and the need to say something ineffable about both of them. No wonder we call for madder music and more wine. No wonder New Year's Eve is such a trial. And you thought it was the paper hats and noise makers that got you down?

Well, Georgetown had a pretty good year, all things considered. We got a lot of brick sidewalks to replace the old concrete ones, housing sales went up and everyone discovered winter pansies — which are really just spring pansies except that until a few years ago, no one knew you could plant them in the fall. They won't look good the whole winter, but then, who does?

A lot of fancy new shops opened on upper Wisconsin Avenue, indicating some kind of faith in the neighborhood and hope for the future. M Street looks tidier, and the perception of crime has gentled a little. A little — it's 1995, remember, and not 1940. Georgetown Park remains a more interesting mall than most, and the shop life around the canal is diverse and spirited. The waterfront at Washington Harbour is the most fashionable and salubrious place to walk up and down since jaded British peers went to Nice to stroll along the Promenade des Anglais a century ago.

Visually, Georgetown is still a knockout. The noble river, the funky canal and its charming towpath, the long vistas up and down 18th century streets — you can't beat it. And the street life. Vibrant, that's what it is, and teeming. Sort of like Calcutta, minus the cows, sort of like Victorian England, sort of like late 20th century America.

Here's my vision for a New Year in Georgetown — maybe not this new year, but sometime soon. Picture Wisconsin Avenue with brick sidewalks, well-planted, well-tended tree boxes, handsome street furniture, cheerful window boxes or pots of flowers outside shop doors. And picture, too, a lively, courteous populace and free-flowing traffic. Sounds pretty good, doesn't it?

In the meantime, go for a winter walk and end up at Dean & DeLuca. There, amid the succulent sights and scents, dream of Provence or a Tuscan hill town. And reflect for a moment on just how fortunate we are, as the year turns, to be living here and now in our own pleasant little village.

– January 1995

Babylon on the Potomac

THINK of any glittering jewel of a city, past or present — the bustle of crowds, the varied shops, the pulse of life beating up, the succulent eateries, the lighted windows a stay against winter and the dark. Lively cities equal people plus setting. And *voila*! Here in Georgetown we have both.

On December 8, the holiday season opened with a nautical Parade of Lights as boats proceeded in a stately manner up and down the Potomac, to the obvious delight of the assembled crowd. Pageantry, that's what we need. Other riverfront communities have long enjoyed this kind of thing. Venice has a procession of decorated gondolas on the Grand Canal. Yacht club cruises, traveling in vast numbers, dress up their rigging with a gala display of flags and pennants when entering and leaving harbors. The Thames honors kings and queens with nautical hoopla, and New York has the tall ships. Stirring. They are stirring sights. And ours was, too.

Fanciful boats lit up and in full holiday regalia passed by just as dusk began to fall. Crowd favorites included eight tiny reindeer poised as if to take flight from the bow of a 40-foot cabin cruiser with Santa at the wheel. On a boat disguised as a fire engine complete with moving wheels and full hook and ladder, Snoopy was sitting atop his doghouse.

Adding to the festive atmosphere in Georgetown this past year was the opening of no less than 14 movie theaters — oops, theatres — at Anthony Lanier's new "Incinerator Site" right across K Street from the river. Here a carnival atmosphere now prevails on evenings and weekends. The up-to-the-minute "multiplex" theatre boasts not just the 14 movie screens, but concessions featuring popcorn shrimp, nachos grande, funnel cake and twirly fries, as well as fried chicken, pizza and on and on.

This brand new Georgetown attraction is very well attended. (That means very many people going to the movies and also many very helpful attendants.) It is usually easy to park in the building, with a special theatre rate for four hours — time for a movie and dinner. As a byproduct of the new theater's popularity, restaurants in Georgetown are booming.

Looking out from the theatre over the once and future Waterfront Park, you can see seagulls padding around on the damp grass, the Potomac going about its stately business, sweetly flowing. This view of the river from Georgetown is always a treat. Now the calm outdoor scene contrasts nicely with the busy scene within.

It's all splendid indeed, even if it puts one in mind of the Duchess of Richmond's Ball on the eve of the Battle of Waterloo: Amidst the revelry, the perception of struggle yet to come.

– January 2003

More Than Just a
Good Address

FROM our earliest houses — dating from the beginning of the 18th century — through the mansions and townhouses of the Georgian, early Federal and Classical Revival periods up to the florid structures of the Gilded Age after the Civil War, Georgetown houses are nothing less than a record of American architecture. We have grand formal houses with stately lawns and big trees standing next to small houses set flush with the sidewalk. We are a neighborhood with a reputation for being culturally savvy, reasonably intelligent and justly famous for our vibrant social scene. And we have worked to keep these attributes.

Throughout its history, citizen action has saved Georgetown. Sometimes it was necessary to see the charm that lay beneath the dilapidation. We have withstood the depredations of the years, weathering periods of neglect, then enjoying the headiness that goes with being back in fashion. Repeatedly, we have had to work hard to preserve and restore our architectural heritage.

When there have been threats, residents have looked at our framework of handsome and important 18th and 19th century houses and have come together to protect what we have here. The result is this splendid enclave that we call home. "Georgetown's survival," according to our premiere historian, Mary Mitchell, "is nothing short of an urban miracle."

Supposing an errant breeze came by and blew aside the gauzy curtain that separates the present from the past and we were back in the Georgetown of 1878. Through this time warp we would see open fields, orchards, cows grazing, lambs amid the buttercups, livery stables, gravel walks, vineyards, quincunxes, bowers. Bicycles were introduced at the 1876 Centennial Exposition and rapidly became enormously popular. Under the big trees in a leisurely southern atmosphere we would have organ grinders, balloon men and pony rides with mama. Children rolling hoops. An easier time? Maybe. But then again maybe not.

If it all seemed calmer, like a sepia photograph, it wasn't all a picture book world. Medical care was still primitive. There were fearsome slums and people living in dreadful conditions in service alleys. Often these were the people who worked as domestics in the big houses scattered about on both sides of Wisconsin Avenue. On the east side of Wisconsin around 28th Street was an area known as Herring Hill. Everybody sold seafood, and the yards are to this day full of oyster shells. You could swim in the river and get baptized in Rock Creek. Milk was delivered by horse and wagon in glass bottles with the cream on top.

Is it better to look back at the past or forward to the future? We live in the reflected glory of the great old houses of Georgetown — Evermay, Tudor Place, Dumbarton Oaks, Mackall Square, Cooke's Row; the Houses Bodisco, Dodge, Halcyon, Laird-Dunlop, Longdon, and Prospect; the Carpenter's Gothic house at the top of 31st Street. And this list just skims the surface.

The Citizens Association of Georgetown has been around a while. Not as long as Evermay, where we celebrated its 125th anniversary, but still a long time. It has taken on the continuing problems of newness, bigness, freeways, noise, pollution, commercialism, and encroaching public institutions. With our mixture of down home and swank, quiet classiness and modern striving, Georgetown, is, after all, not so much a place as a state of mind.

– October 2003

"The years are passing..."

THE story goes that Napoleon's mother used to wander around the Tuileries muttering "This will never last." She was on to something, something that could be a theme for musings on life right now in our little global village.

It's the time of year when we tend to think about these things: the fleeting nature of our triumphs (alas) and the transient nature of our trials (we hope). In spite of our valiant efforts not to do so, we think about time and its little hurrying feet. Now is the season for the dreaded taking of stock, not the kind on the big board, but the kind of stocktaking that involves a cold-eyed appraisal of where we are on our allotted time lines and how we are doing. Putting the wraiths of one year to rest, picking up the threads let go over the holidays and refashioning them into a life for the coming year. Fresh slates. New beginnings. High resolve. Difficult, but let's put this into perspective.

Here in Georgetown in the interior of the block bounded by P, O, 30th and 31st Streets, there is a magnificent stand of *Metasequoia glyptostroboides*, otherwise known as the Dawn Redwood. In 1941, fossils of this "extinct" tree were found in Japan, and then — later that same year — specimens were found growing wild in China. In 1944, the Arnold Arboretum sent an expedition to China to collect seeds, which subsequently were shared with botanical gardens around the world. The discovery and dispersal of this fossil tree was greeted with delight. The Dawn Redwood has been growing and reproducing itself for 50 million years.

Now while that's a nice story, it's just too much perspective for our purposes here. As the years of this millennium dwindle down to a precious few, we need a more human scale. We need to place ourselves at the turning of the year, at the waning of the 20th century, at the countdown to the millennium. After all, this is the only millennium, we have ever known. Reflect for a minute on life in 1996 and be grateful. These are vintage years, as Frank Sinatra might have put it. And, as Paul Simon knew, they are slipsliding away.

In *Speak, Memory*, Vladimir Nabokov wrote: "They are passing, posthaste, posthaste, the gliding years...The years are passing, my dear, and presently no one will know what you and I know." Well, ever singing march we onward.

Driving down Wisconsin Avenue, at the top of the hill by the library, with twilight coming on, one sees vast imposing gray clouds piling up over the river, which spreads out before us like a diorama. We drivers, happily isolated in our snug little cars, continue our silent ritual cursing of each other for left turns and other breaches of the public trust. The lights come on. It's cold, but not that cold. It's dark and bleak, but not that dark and bleak. And we are almost home.

– January 1997

100

Edith Schafer

Edith Nalle Schafer has been writing her column, "Aspects of Georgetown," for the newsletter of the Citizens Association of Georgetown since 1994. A native of Philadelphia, she attended Vassar College and graduated from Bryn Mawr College. After winning *Vogue* magazine's *Prix de Paris*, she lived for a time in Paris, but left France and the fashion world for a job in publishing in New York City. Her previous books include *Our Remarkable Memory* and *Literary Circles of Washington*. She and her husband, John Schafer, have been active in community affairs in Georgetown since the early 1960's. The Schafers' grandchildren are now third-generation Georgetowners.